Enter Through the Narrow Gate

Essays on the Spiritual Journey of Life

by
Richard Gribble, CSC

PublishAmerica
Baltimore

© 2010 by Richard Gribble, CSC
All rights reserved. No part of this book may be reproduced, stored in a retrieval system or transmitted in any form or by any means without the prior written permission of the publishers, except by a reviewer who may quote brief passages in a review to be printed in a newspaper, magazine or journal.

First printing

PublishAmerica has allowed this work to remain exactly as the author intended, verbatim, without editorial input.

Hardcover 978-1-4560-2231-0
Softcover 978-1-4560-2230-3
PUBLISHED BY PUBLISHAMERICA, LLLP
www.publishamerica.com
Baltimore

Printed in the United States of America

Dedication

The narrow gate that leads to life is not a simple path, but rather is generally marked with adversity and pain. In my life I have been privileged to witness the faith journeys of many who have struggled mightily but have never given into despair. These people have been a model for me in how to deal with the adversities of life and transform them into life-giving experiences. The Virgin Mary was a woman who knew great pain and suffering because she walked the narrow path to life. She has been an example to countless people over Christian history. One woman who has walked the narrow road in two cultures, and followed Mary's lead, is my friend Sister Tania. It is to her that this book of reflections is dedicated.

Table of Contents

Dedication 3
Preface 7

Section I: God Challenges Us

Introduction...13
Baptism: The Call to Discipleship...........................15
If You Really Love God—Show Me!.......................20
Living For Others..24
Accepting the Lord Once Again..............................28
Reaching Out to Others..32
God Gives Us a Chance 36
Allowing Jesus to Feed Us......................................40
Who Do You Say That I Am? 44
The Challenge of Tough Love 49
Reconciliation: The Journey of Faith 53
Stewards of God's Gifts 57
Our Commitment to the Lord.................................61
Welcoming God in One Another 65
An Agent of Salvation...69
Discovering God's Will 73
What We Do Matters..78
Carrying the Tradition..82

Section II: Daily Human Struggles

Introduction...89
Encountering Christ the Merciful One....................91
What Are You Willing to Do For Me? 97
Preparing the Way of the Lord 102

Allowing God to Change Us 107
Loyalty to God or the World? 111
Dying to New Life 114
Using Authority Properly......................................117
Making Room for Christ 121
Feeding Each Other..124
Life Comes From the Cross 128
Getting Involved With God...................................132
God Can Complete Mission Impossible................135
Agape: The Highest Form of Love 144

Section III: The Presence of God in the World

Introduction...151
Advocates for the Body of Christ 153
Reliance Upon God..159
"Speak, Lord, Your Servant is Listening"...............162
Nothing is Too Difficult for God 170
God Is Our Permanent Hope 173
Jesus: A Spiritual Revolution 176
Take Care—Be Ready 181
God Welcomes All 184
Piloting With God..188
God's Word Blossoms Forth 191
Acting on Our Belief..194
God is Present in All that We Do 198
Those Who Seek the Truth Hear God's Voice.......203

Preface

"Enter through the narrow gate; for the gate is wide and the road is easy that leads to destruction, and there are many who take it. For the gate is narrow and the road is hard that leads to life, and there are few who find it." (Matthew 7:13-14) St. Matthew reports these words of Jesus toward the end of the famous "Sermon on the Mount." The Lord wanted his followers to know that discipleship is not the easy road in life; it is the one that is cluttered, strewn with obstacles, and at times seemingly unnavigable. But despite the difficulties it is the only path that will lead us home to be with God. In a very succinct but powerful way Jesus has instructed all his followers on what is necessary to discover and walk the proper road. While we need not seek the rough path, we should not be surprised when it finds us. More importantly we must not shrink from following this road, for only in this way can we find eternal life

Contemporary society seeks to be comfortable and to avoid pain at all costs. This attitude often manifests itself in our reluctance to enter into opportunities that might be challenging or difficult, even though we might grow in the process. We don't want to take the chance; we prefer to take the easy route, the way of comfortableness toward which society directs us. In the process we often miss opportunities, that although difficult, might just be the avenue that will bring us to life. Most people agree that the accomplishment of difficult tasks and finding solutions to problematic situations brings us growth. This process of growth is not painless, but many of the greatest lessons in life are learned the hard way. We often discover much about who we are and what we can do from "the school of hard knocks." The famous twentieth-century British writer G. K. Chesterton said it well, "The Christian ideal has not been tried and found wanting. It has been found difficult, and left untried."

All people along the journey of life will experience circumstances that challenge them to take the more difficult road. With society whispering in our ear of our need to take the easy route, we initially think ourselves foolish to even consider this difficult trek. Why would one intentionally cause oneself pain and suffering? Its appears so contrary to "normal" thinking to pursue any course but the path of least resistance. But what the world considers "normal" and operative, is often in conflict with the Christian ideal. While it might seem today that the purpose of life is to "go for the gusto," find ideal happiness, and pursue your personal dreams, Christianity paints a very different picture, one that considers suffering as a badge of honor. Jesus did not want the cross. In fact, the night before he died Jesus called out to God, "My Father, if it is possible, let this cup pass from me; yet not what I want but what you want." Later he added, "Your will be done." (Matthew 26:39b, 42c) If we are true disciples of Jesus, then we can expect no better than the Master we strive to follow. If we place our hope and trust in God, then the narrow way, with all its problems and obstacles, becomes the holy way, the course of learning, and the path that will lead us home to God.

This book is divided into three sections that look at the narrow path in different ways. Essays on "The Challenge of God" outline the many ways our Lord presents us with obstacles that are opportunities for growth. In the section on "Daily Human Struggles" we are confronted with how society and the reality of the world can sometimes provide growth through pain and suffering. The third section, "The Presence of God in the World" offers hope to the weary traveler that God is as near as your own person and will always be present to assist one along the road of life.

The composition of these essays in many ways reveals my personal spiritual journey. While each person's path is unique, I hope that the insight I have discovered through prayer and experience may be helpful as you walk your own path. The life Jesus gave us is a gift filled with wonder and pregnant with possibilities. May the gift of life given us be shared with others as we pass through the narrow gate to eternal life.

Richard Gribble, CSC

Section I
God Challenges Us

Introduction

One of the strongest memories of my undergraduate days at the United States Naval Academy in Annapolis, Maryland was the twice annual necessity to successfully negotiate an obstacle course. This challenge, together with a mile run under six minutes and an "applied strength" test consisting of pull ups, sit-ups, and dips on a parallel bar, were a tripartite fall and spring ritual to determine physical strength and endurance. While the run and applied strength required some work, it was the obstacle course which was my great challenge. A series of cargo nets, walls, sand pits and balancing beams presented a severe challenge, especially for those of short stature, to finish under the allowable time and not hurt oneself in the process. I had to practice and plan for that semi-annual test, but even with all my planning there were unexpected things that came along—inclement weather, other midshipmen impeding my progress, and the ever present possibility of falling, slipping or simply failure. The challenge was great; it was my task to accept it and do my best.

God challenges us in many ways each day. Some of these challenges arrive, like my semi-annual obstacle course run, in a way and timeliness that allows us to plan, and others arrive without warning. Many times we shy away from challenge, feeling that we are not ready for it, the reality that we might have to change, or the fear of failure. In some cases, however, we have no choice. Events may come about that we simply cannot avoid; we either deal with the challenge or we give up. While challenge, in all its forms, causes us to stretch our abilities, perceptions, or ideas, it also provides us with a path for growth. They say in sports, "no pain, not gain." If we are not willing to go beyond our level of physical comfortableness we will never run faster, block better, or hit harder and further. But if we can motivate ourselves to go beyond our present limits, then the possibilities are endless. Such is the nature of God's challenge. While there often may be pain, engaging the challenges of God will allow us to grow, become better people of faith and be stronger in order to endure future challenges. Then we can help others who may be struggling.

The reflections in this section address many challenges that come to us from God. In each case we have the option of accepting or rejecting the challenge, but it we wish to grow closer to the Lord, we really have only one option. We have the significant challenge to be true disciples of Christ and follow where he directs us. The need to demonstrate love, even in the most difficult circumstances, is another significant challenge. We are also asked to forgive and be forgiven, welcome others, especially the stranger, outcast and those on the margins of society, cast out fear from our lives, and live for others as Jesus lived and died for us. The challenges that God sends our way will many times be difficult, but those who persevere and accept these as opportunities for growth will be better for it in the end. Let us answer the challenges of God and find fulfillment, personal growth, and satisfaction in the process.

Baptism: The Call to Discipleship

"And Jesus came and said to them, 'All authority in heaven and on earth has been given to me. Go therefore and make disciples of all nations, baptizing them in the name of the Father and of the Son and of the Holy Spirit, and teaching them to obey everything that I have commanded you. And remember, I am with you always, to the end of the age." (Matthew 28:18-20) The words of Jesus echo with a command, a privilege, and a challenge. The Lord has challenged us to go forward as disciples and share his message with others. As God's children through baptism we are privileged to share God's life, but this privilege does not come without the consequent command to go forward. Baptism, the sacrament which unites all Christians in one family also unites us in the common call to discipleship.

The concept of baptism as a rite is rather straight forward, but the responsibilities that come with this sacrament are more complex. We all know that baptism makes us children of God and all the privileges that come with this elect position. Most people are not equally knowledgeable, however, about what baptism requires, or possibly we refuse to accept the responsibilities that comes with the privilege. Baptism is a call to discipleship—but what exactly is discipleship?

Discipleship may be defined in many ways, but three principal aspects are crucial. To be a disciple first means to be a follower. Through baptism we become followers of Jesus and members of the Church. Baptism next calls us to ministry, the work of a disciple. Lastly, discipleship requires that we become evangelists in response to Jesus' command to go and make disciples of all nations.

The process of being a follower of Jesus necessitates our total dedication to his principles and message. We cannot be a follower some days and one who goes it alone on others. Our mind must be fixed on the Lord. St. Peter puts it well, "And Baptism, which this prefigured, now saves you—not as a removal of dirt from the body, but as an appeal to God for a good conscience, through the resurrection pf Jesus Christ." (I Peter 3:21). Baptism is more than an act, it is a promise. Whether we knew it or not our baptism bound us to Christ and the Church. Thus, our attitude must be such as to seek union, with God and God's people.

Following Jesus is not easy; nobody said it would be. Dietrich Bonhoeffer, the famous Lutheran theologian who was executed by the Nazis at the end of World War II, knew that the price to be a true follower would be high. In his famous book *The Cost of Discipleship* Bonhoeffer says that to be a disciple of Jesus will cost us everything in this life, but lead to eternal life. Bonhoeffer knew and believed what the Scriptures say concerning our baptism into Christ's death and how it leads to life. St. Paul wrote, "When you were buried with him in Baptism, you were also raised with him through faith in the power of God, who raised him from the dead." (Colossians 2:12)

Discipleship requires us to minister to God's people. The tendency for many is to think that only certain people are called to ministry—one must have a vocation for such work. All the baptized, however, are called to work in the vineyard of the Lord. As Scripture states, "The harvest is plentiful but the laborers are few; therefore ask the Lord of the harvest to send out laborers into his harvest." (Luke 10:2) We are the workers;

we are the Body of Christ. We are members of the priesthood of believers. Whatever our vocation, the single life, marriage and family, or religious life, we are all one through baptism. Again St. Paul has written, "For in the spirit we are all baptized into one body—Jews, Greeks, slaves or free." (I Corinthians 12:13a). As members of the one body, as brothers and sisters in the Lord, our ministry is a service to God and God's people.

Within the Body of Christ we minister in specialized ways. Marriage places emphasis on ministry to spouse and children. Professionals can transform their daily work into ministry by an attitude of service to others. Single people also demonstrate ministry in their association with people around them. The ordained priesthood, a special invitation to discipleship, is a vehicle to minister in ways, if done well, which can touch many people. Priests, through the sacraments and preaching, minister to all God's people and provide a special face to the presence of God in our world. This is the essential work of discipleship.

Evangelization is the third important aspect of discipleship. Jesus commands us to be evangelists, to go forth and spread his message. When we think of evangelization the image of the street-corner preacher comes to mind. Sermons of Hell-fire and brimstone and selling the faith door-to-door are other popular images. Evangelization is practiced in these ways, but there are less overt and more common ways in which we bring others closer to God, which is the essential ministry of the evangelist.

Evangelization is practiced in the active life of the minister. As has already been mentioned, ministry and service are not optional works for the Christian; all are called to work in God's vineyard. How many of us have been touched by the works and service of others? When we see someone who reaches out to another, like the late Mother Theresa and her Missionaries of Charity, we are challenged to go the extra mile for those who need our assistance. The actions of others force us to act; their service becomes an instance of evangelization. Active ministry and service to others is something in which we can participate each day. There are formal ministries in the Church and the community, but more commonly service is performed in everyday events which few think is significant. Courtesy in our manner of life, calmness in a time of strife, using conciliation over argumentation in time of conflict are all ways of demonstrating service to others and ministry in God's Kingdom on earth.

Another important method of evangelization is the process of reconciliation. The ability to admit one's brokenness, especially before another, is an act of evangelization. How many times have we been inspired and had our hearts lifted by seeing another turn away from evil and begin a new path which leads to God? Baptism is a rebirth into the life of repentance. Scripture states that John the Baptist came as a precursor of the Lord to provide a baptism of repentance for the forgiveness of sins (Mark 1:4; Like 3:3, Acts 13:24). When one turns away from sin and begins anew, the value of such an act is incalculable. Repentance and reconciliation require courage and provide a challenge for others to seek a similar road in their lives.

Reconciliation as a means of evangelization and discipleship is most strongly seen in the Sacrament of Penance. The courage to honestly face one's human brokenness, imperfection, and sinfulness is of immeasurable witness value to others. Like the reaction of the forgiving father in parable of the Prodigal Son (Luke 15:11-32), we are moved in emotion and brought closer to God by the humility of a fellow human. Moreover, the sacrament itself, which celebrates God's forgiveness and our reconciliation with God's people, the Body of Christ, empowers us through a renewed spirit to bring God's message of love to all. Thus, reconciliation becomes a vehicle for evangelization.

Baptism as a call to discipleship is an active sacrament; it is anything but passive. This first sacrament calls us to be followers, ministers and evangelists. We must live the vocation of holiness to which we have all been called. Our call is to be members with all the privileges that come with being part of God's family. Our membership gives us responsibilities as well. We must go forth in an active manner to do God's work in our world. Baptism is the original call to a life which seeks to bring others closer to God. May the baptism which we all share, our common denominator in the faith, allow us to be disciples and show the face of God to others.

Question: How well do I fulfill my responsibilities as a baptized Christian?

Scripture Passage: "When they [James and John] had brought their boats to shore, they left everything and followed him." (Luke 5:11)

Prayer: Lord, help me to be your disciple in all that I say and do.

If You Really Love God—Show Me!

William Barclay, a famous commentator on Sacred Scripture, tells a story of an Orthodox Jewish rabbi, imprisoned in a cruel regime, who was barely able to survive so meager were the rations of food and water that he was given. As an Orthodox Jew he scrupulously maintained the letter of the law with respect to dietary rules and cleanliness. Each day when he received his meager portion of food and water he made certain that he completed all the ritual washings before eating and ate only those things that the law did not forbid. In the process he almost always used up his ration of drink in washing and nearly wasted away from the lack of food. Fortunately he got out of prison in time, for if his time was any longer he would have died of thirst and malnutrition, all because he loved the Law!

There is a story told by a missionary in New Guinea. An old man, who was a recent convert to Christianity, regularly came to the mission hospital every day to read the gospels to the patients. One day the man was having great difficulty reading and, thus, a doctor examined him and discovered that he was going blind and would probably be so in a year or two at most. After this revelation the old man was not found at the hospital; no one knew what had happened to him. Eventually one of the missionaries found him and brought the mission doctor to him. The old man explained that he had not come to the hospital because he was busy memorizing the gospels while he could still see. "Soon I'll be back at the hospital," he told the doctor, "and I will continue my work of teaching the gospel message to the patients."

One day in 1942 a prisoner escaped from the notorious Nazi death camp at Auschwitz in Poland. The camp commander, irritated at this bold action, decided to teach the other prisoners a sobering lesson. He selected at random ten men and scheduled them to be executed in public. One of the men selected was a family man, a fact that was noted by a Franciscan priest, Maximilian Kolbe, who was also a prisoner. The priest stepped forward and offered to take the family man's place. The camp commander was stunned but accepted the offer. Maximilian Kolbe died so another might live. Kolbe's courage was an illustration of Jesus' challenge: "No one has greater love than this, to lay down one's life for one's friends." (John 15:13)

These three stories all speak of the love through sacrifice, sacrifice of self to the law of God, and sacrifice of self for the needs and lives of others. Scripture challenges us to consider how much we love God and our neighbor and to demonstrate that love to all. God gave Moses, the great liberator of the Israelites, the Law, the stone tablets upon which were written the Ten Commandments. The Law was critical to the Hebrews for it formed their whole way of thinking and living. The importance of the Law was expressed by Moses: "Hear, therefore, O Israel, and observe them [the dictates of the law] diligently, so that it may go well with you, and so that you may multiply greatly in a land flowing with milk and honey." (Deuteronomy 6:3) The first and most important commandment was clear: "You shall love the Lord your God with all your heart, and with all your soul, and with all your might." (Deuteronomy 6:5) For the Hebrews nothing was more important than this rule. In the Gospels Jesus repeats Moses words, but goes one important step further. He agrees that love of God with one's whole heart, mind, soul, and strength was fundamental, but in explicating "The Golden Rule" He says, "You shall love your neighbor as yourself." (Mark 12:31)

Few disagree with the ideas expressed in the Golden Rule. People of good will love God and at least make an effort to love their neighbor, but how do we truly show we manifest our love for God and neighbor? To what length will we go to demonstrate what we say we believe as practicing Christians? In the Broadway musical "My Fair Lady" Eliza Doolittle, fed up and exasperated with the protestations of love found in letters and verbal expressions of "I love you" from her boyfriend Freddy, sings the song, "Show Me!" She says that she is sick of words and talk. "If there is any love burning in your heart," she sings, "show me!" God might ask the same thing of us. If we truly love God what are we doing in concrete ways to demonstrate it to him and our neighbor? The New Testament is filled with references of how Jesus demonstrated his love for us through his death and resurrection; he constantly stands ready to intercede to the Father on our behalf. Are we ready to offer ourselves for God and our neighbor?

How have we truly demonstrated our love for God and God's people, our neighbors? When was the last time we stuck up for someone who was being maligned or unjustly criticized in a conversation within our family or at work? How many times recently have we intentionally gone out of our way to assist another person, possibly at great personal risk or to the detriment of our own advancement? When given the opportunity to defend God and/or the Church against the many attacks they daily receive from the media, anti-Catholics, even those within the Christian community who are angry, concerning issues like abortion and euthanasia, did you take the occasion seriously and make a case for God? Do we love God sufficiently that we will make daily prayer, weekly Mass, and regular celebration of the sacrament of penance normative in our lives and refuse to make excuses when we fail? Do we love God so much that we would have the courage to give up all we are and hope to be so that God's Kingdom may be advanced in our world?

The Golden Rule, to love God with our whole heart, soul, mind, and strength, and our neighbor as ourself, will be only a pious platitude unless we are ready to truly show God that we mean what we say. Let us, therefore, critically examine our lives and ask the hard question of what we have done lately to truly manifest in concrete ways our love for God. Our inner search may discover things we wish not to admit, but if we clear out the doubts and uncertainties then we can fill the void with a new resolve to love beyond all measure and without counting the cost. Our reward will be eternal life.

Question: When was the last time I outwardly demonstrated my faith and commitment to Christ when challenged to do so?

Scripture Passage: "If we have died with him, we will also live with him; if we endure, we will also reign with him." (II Timothy 2:11-12)

Prayer: Loving Father, may I never shy away from the challenges of faith that you send to me.

Living For Others

How does one define the concept of divinity? We might begin by some description of the aspects of the being divine. The divine is infinite; the divine is omnipotent and omniscient. These ideas help to describe divinity, but they don't do much to define it. We need something to which we can relate in order to understand the concept of the divine.

The best answer to our original question is to speak in terms of participation in the divine. Thus, one can ask the question, how can one seek to be divine-like? An answer that appeals to many is, to the degree that we live for others is the degree in which we participate in the divine. We can give many examples of this idea. One dramatic example of such commitment was manifested one year in the annual "Iron Man" competition in Hawaii. In this annual athletic test of strength and endurance, where one swims two miles, bikes over 150 miles and then finishes with a 26 mile marathon run, one competitor participated in and finished the race with his crippled son strapped to his back. He ran, biked, and swam for his son.

There are more famous examples of living for others. In his famous "I have a Dream" speech before the Washington Mall in August 1963, Martin Luther King, Jr. expressed the hopes which he shared and lived for in creating a more just world for all. John F. Kennedy, in his inaugural address said, "Ask not what your country can do for you, ask what you can do for your country."

There are incalculable routine and ordinary ways in which people live for others, yet maybe they are the most profound because they are everyday events. People who donate time to work in a soup line, a youngster who shares her sandwich with a child who has none, parents who sacrifice time, energy, and resources out of love for their children. To the extent that we live for others, is the extent in which we participate in the divine.

Jesus was divine and thus he lived totally for others. The image of Jesus as the Good Shepherd, described in John's Gospel (10:11-18), powerfully illustrates how the Lord lives for others by laying down his life. John sets up a contrast between the hired hand and Jesus. The hired hand does what he does merely for the reward that will come with his service; he makes no investment and has no true interest. When danger approaches the hired hand runs; there is no reason to stay. The hired hand must protect himself; he does not worry about others. Jesus, on the other hand, is the one who cares. He lays down his life for others. This is done freely; it is not taken from him. Jesus' care goes out to all. As he says, "I have other sheep that do not belong to this fold." (John 10:16a) Jesus will lay down his life for them as well.

The Lord was not one who looked for fame in his earthly life. Worldly recognition was not essential to his mission. Although he was rejected, as the New Testament states, he became the pillar, the cornerstone upon which the Church was founded. Jesus was not recognized for who he was, but nevertheless we have been recognized as God's children. Jesus lived totally for others. He gave his life, rose from the dead, and proved his divinity!

To the extent we live for others is the extent we participate in the divinity of Christ. Living for others begins with an attitude. First, we must treat all people with human dignity. We are called to care for all people with respect and love. Secondly, we must treat all people equally. Race, religion, sex, creed—these should have no bearing on the way we view and interact with people. We are all brothers and sisters, children of God, equal in God's eyes. Lastly, we must show fraternity in our relationship with others. Living in community, sharing our lives, thoughts and prayers—this is being fraternal, this is living for others.

Living for others continues with our actions. Through our common baptismal call we are asked to lead lives of service, especially to the poor and those who have little or no voice in our world. We are challenged to lead lives of ministry. It may be formal ministry as a full time person at a parish or Church-related organization. For most, however, our lives of ministry are less formal, but equally important. In the Church we live for others by our ministry, whether it is participation in the liturgical celebration, membership in groups that aid the poor or assisting with the annual parish fundraiser. In the community we live for others through local government, fraternal organizations and volunteer work. Living lives of self-giving and sacrifice is the essence of ministry. Parents living for their children, families visiting elder members in hospitals and nursing homes, people giving their time and talent so others may share their abundance—these are all examples of living for others, that is participating in the divine.

Jesus, our brother, friend, and Lord lived totally for others. Jesus freely laid down his life for us. Why? Because he loved us, because he wanted to share himself with us. Jesus the good shepherd asks us to live our lives in a similar manner. Jesus asks us to live for others in attitude, in word, and in action. Jesus asks us to love, especially those we find most difficult to love. Jesus asks us to lay down our lives, through service, ministry, and sacrifice. If we live for others, if we love, if we lay down our lives, we participate in the divinity of Jesus and we make the resurrection a reality each day of our lives.

Question: When was the last time I sacrificed my need for the needs of others?

Scripture Passage: "All who exalt themselves will be humbled, and all who humble themselves will be exalted." (Matthew 23:12)

Prayer: Lord, help me to share my life with others as you did for us.

Accepting the Lord Once Again

He came softly, unobserved and yet, strange to say, everyone knew him. The time was the fifteenth century; the place was Seville in Spain. He came to announce peace and to proclaim the good news. He came to teach and to cure; He came to bring the light. As he walked by the cathedral, a funeral procession for a little seven year old girl was just beginning to form. He heard the sobs and pleas of the girl's mother. Moved with compassion he asked the bearers of the funeral bier to halt. He touched the girl; she was raised to life once again.

The local Cardinal Archbishop of the city heard about this event. Such displays of power were not to be tolerated. Such action led to faith which would only be dashed in the cruelty of the world. He was thus thrown into prison as a common criminal. In prison he was questioned by the chief or Grand Inquisitor of the city, "Why have you come? We don't need you here!" The prisoner made no response. The Inquisitor thus continued his harangue, questioning the prisoner about his time in the desert, at the beginning of his ministry, when he was tempted with the great luxuries of power, wealth and prestige. "You were a fool," said the Inquisitor. "You should have accepted Satan's offer! Why are you so bent on self-destruction? Why did you choose miracle, mystery and authority over power, wealth, and prestige? There is no longer a need to believe in you and what you bring. Go away, you are not welcome here." This time the prisoner did answer, not with words, but with actions. He embraced the Inquisitor, kissed him, and walked out of the prison. He moved on to offer himself to another group at another time in history.

Fydor Dostoyevsky's famous tale, "The Grand Inquisitor," in his equally celebrated book, *The Brothers Karamazov*, describes the rejection of Christ who has come to bring light, goodness, and peace to a world who needs him, but refuses to accept His presence. In a similar way Scripture speaks of what Jesus brought to the world and how he was rejected.

The second section of Isaiah (chapters 35-55), known as Deutero-Isaiah, was addressed to the Hebrew people in exile in Babylon. The people had little hope; they lived with the thought that they had been rejected by God. However, in chapter 52:2-3 Isaiah prophesies a new beginning for the nation: "Shake yourself from the dust, rise up, O captive Jerusalem; loose the bonds from your neck, O captive Zion! For thus says the Lord: You were sold for nothing, and you shall be redeemed without money." This new life for the people will restore Zion. The Lord will come to the people announcing peace, bearing good news, comforting the people, and announcing salvation. The Lord will, thus, provide all that the people need to renew their lives and live as God's people.

The prologue of John's Gospel (1:1-18) is one of the most famous passages in Scripture. Possibly more has been written about this pericope than any other. We are told by the evangelist that Jesus was the Word made flesh; he is the presence of God who dwells among us. Jesus was the light, a favorite metaphor of St. John's writings, a light which no darkness can overcome. Jesus, the Son of God, brought his message of salvation, hope, and love.

We know, however, as Scripture clearly indicates, that Jesus was not accepted by the very people to whom he came. St. John says, "He came to what was his own, and his own people did not accept him." (1:11) The Jews expected a warrior Messiah who would restore the Davidic kingship and with it greatness in stature to Israel. The people misread the message of the prophets and rejected Christ and his message.

Have things changed that much in 2000 years? We look at our world and wonder if Jesus has made any progress in His struggle to find acceptance among the peoples of the earth? Thousands suffer famine because the light is not accepted. Violence eclipses peace in our streets. Ethnic cleansing was used as a rationale for atrocities perpetrated by the Serbs against Muslims in Bosnia-Herzegovina and Albanians in Kosovo. Racial tensions continue to plague many nations and make international headlines. Where is the good news; where is the comfort and salvation of God?

With all the problems and bad news we may wonder what significance Jesus' message has for us today. The answer to the question and the solution to the world's ills are totally up to us. The message of Jesus must be applied today in order to find relevance and meaning! If we do nothing to make Jesus' presence meaningful for our world, then like the Grand Inquisitor, Christ's rejection will continue. Jesus brought hope; he brought light so that a people in darkness would never be fearful again. It is up to us!

St. Paul's image of the body in I Corinthians tells us that God acts in our world through our hands and feet and speaks through our tongues. We, therefore, are the light, the hope, the bearers of Good News. As Paul says, we are the Body of Christ. We have a responsibility to pass on the gifts Jesus brings to others. We begin with ourselves and then move to others. Let us respond to the challenge and answer the call to bring Jesus to others in all that we say and do.

Question: Do I welcome or reject Christ in my day-to-day activities?

Scripture Passage: "Whoever listens to you listens to me, and whoever rejects you rejects me, and whoever rejects me rejects the one who sent me." (Luke 10:16)

Prayer: Lord Jesus, help me bid welcome to you through my assistance to others.

Reaching Out to Others

Once in a far-off land there was a great king whose dominion extended far and wide. His power and authority were absolute. One day a young man, a commoner, committed a grave offense against the king. In response the king and his counselors gathered together to determine what should be done. They decided that since the offense was so grave and had been committed by a commoner against someone so August as the king, the only punishment that would satisfy justice was death. The king's son, the crown prince, however, interceded on the young offender's behalf—you see they were best friends. The prince spoke with his father and the counselors; the debate grew rather heated. In the end the king declared, "The offender must pay a price for his offense. I decree that he must carry a heavy burden up Temple Mountain. If he survives the ordeal he shall live!"

The prince again interceded for his friend. He knew the burden of which his father spoke was the weight of death and he knew his friend would not be able to carry it. Thus the prince declared, "Royal blood has been offended, therefore, only royal blood can pay the price." So the prince shouldered the heavy burden himself, and with his friend trailing behind him, he began the ascent of the mountain. The task was very difficult. The higher the prince climbed the heavier the burden became.

The prince slipped and stumbled several times, but he always managed to right himself and keep going. When the two friends first saw the summit, their goal, the prince collapsed from sheer exhaustion. He said to his friend, "In order for justice to be served the price must be paid." The young man understood the prince and, thus, he shouldered the burden himself and, now with the prince following, managed to climb the rest of the way to the summit. When the two friends reached their goal, the prince, with his last ounces of strength, lifted the burden high over his head and then died.

The king, observing all these events from below, declared, "Justice has been completed." Then with his great power he returned his son to life. The prince, now returned to life, said, "Not so, not yet. Justice has not been served. Royal blood received help along the way!" The king had to agree. He pardoned the young offender and the two best friends lived happily ever after.[1]

This powerful tale teaches us a very important message. We learn that God will always do the divine part in reaching out and shouldering the pains and burdens of the world. But humans must do what mortals can do to assure that justice is served and to build the reign of God in our world. The Scriptures also tells us that we too must stretch out our hands, shoulder the burden, live for others, and in that way imitate the divinity which is Christ.

The Scriptures demonstrate how Jesus broke through conventional wisdom in order to aid others. In Mark 1:40-45 Jesus encounters a leper who says, "If you choose, you can cure me." Jesus does will it. He stretches out his arm and it

---

1 Paraphrased from "The Burden: A Tale of Christ," in John Aurelio, *Colors! Stories of the Kingdom* (New York: Crossroad, 1993), 130-32.

happens, the leper is cured. Jesus took on the pain of the leper; the Lord in a very real way lived for him. Jesus took on the pain of ostracization as depicted so vividly in Scripture.

As many people know the Book of Leviticus is filled with laws made so that the Israelite community could better live its commitment to Yahweh. Chapter 13 is filled with regulations that state how lepers are to be treated. It was probably necessary to place barriers and require lepers to stay outside the community. Jesus, however, breaks through the old law. He stretches out his hand, touches, and heals. Jesus truly lived for others.

One might ask, if Jesus cured one leper, why didn't he cure all the lepers in the area? Could he not have gathered all the lepers in the region, or in all Israel for that matter, stretched our his hand and cured them? Could not have Jesus lifted all the burdens of the world, shouldered them, those that are the weight of death, as the prince shouldered the great burden? We know that Jesus did exactly this on his ascent to Calvary. The weight of death was sin, our sin, and he carried it to death.

But in his dealing with the leper he chose to only cure the one who came to him. Jesus was teaching a lesson. He wanted to show the Jews of his day that they too needed to reach out their hands, and take on the burdens of the lepers around them. Jesus is trying to teach us the same thing. Certainly St. Paul was one who reached out to the lepers of his day. He was the great apostle to the Gentiles, a collective group of lepers in the eyes of the Jews. Yet, he did his best and tried to be all things to all people. As he wrote to the Corinthians (I Corinthians 11:1), "Be imitators of me, as I am of Christ."

It should be no revelation to anyone today that there are plenty of lepers in our society. There may be very few who have the physical disease of leprosy, but there are many lepers, nonetheless. They are found among the marginalized people of our society, those that have been ostracized, shunned, and relegated to the fringes. They are seen in the physically and mentally handicapped, the foreigner, the homeless, the aged, the less educated, the diseased, and sick. Jesus says to us, stretch out your hands, shoulder the burden. Imitate me in my efforts to live for others. In the story "The Burden" the prince lived for his friend and saved him. Likewise Jesus asks us to live for others and in so doing we imitate Him and act divine.

C.S. Lewis used a marvelous image which helps us to understand these ideas. He ofttimes spoke of a sculptor working on a piece of stone. The sculptor chipped and chiseled away and with each chip that flew off the true image of the statue trapped in the stone began to come to greater life. In a similar way, God chips and chisels away on us. The chips that fall off come in the forms of challenges, tasks and burdens. Yet with the successful negotiation of each task or challenge the true you or me becomes more visible; we become more beautiful people.

Let us do our best to stretch out our hands to the lepers of our society, in heart, mind, and action. Let us help Jesus to shoulder the burden; let us do our share. Let us live for others and in that way imitate the divinity of Christ, the one who is brother, friend, and Lord to us all.

Question: Am I willing to shoulder the burden of others or am I too absorbed with my own problems and challenges?

Scripture Passage: "You shall love the Lord your God with all your heart, and with all your soul, and with all your strength, and with all your mind; and your neighbor as yourself." (Luke 10:27)

Prayer: Father, help me to shoulder the cross for others as Jesus, your Son, did for me.

God Gives Us a Chance

Billy Mills, a second lieutenant in the United States Marine Corps, was a good runner, but he wasn't a world class runner—at least that is what everyone thought. In 1964 the United States Olympic track and field team had been selected for the Tokyo games. Three athletes had been chosen through a system of qualifying trials for each event. Originally Billy Mills was not a member of the team, but an injury to one member of the 10,000 meter squad gave Lieutenant Mills a chance for glory, and he would make good on the opportunity.

Atypical to most Olympic track events, the 10,000 meters in 1964 did not require a qualifying race to narrow the field. There were 38 runners entered for the grueling 6.2 miles, 25 laps around the newly constructed red clay track in the Olympic stadium. All would run together, the world class and the unknown.

The race was run on October 14, 1964. Some of the best runners in the world were entered in the field, including the 1960 Olympic champion Pyotr Bolotnikov of the Soviet Union and Ron Clarke, the world record holder from New Zealand. After fifteen laps of the race only four of the 38 competitors had any chance of winning. A little known Tunisian runner, Mohamed Gammoudi, Clarke, Bolotnikov and Billy Mills were ahead of the field running in a tight pack. As an unknown in the sports world, no one ever gave Mills even a thought in this race, yet there he was in a position to possibly win the coveted gold medal. The four lead runners jockeyed for position on the track, still damp from an early morning rain. The final lap of the race approached and the gun was sounded indicating the stretch run. The four lead runners began an all out sprint. Bolotnikov fell back; it was now between the Gammoudi, Clarke, and Mills. The Tunisian forged ahead. With 100 meters to go Billy Mills was ten meters behind. Somehow his adrenalin kicked in and he surged ahead. Mills broke the tape first, eclipsing the Olympic record by 8 seconds. Billy Mills was given a chance; he made good on the opportunity.

The parable of the Good Samaritan (Luke 10:25-27) presents a situation where we could ask ourselves the question, "If we were given a special chance, how would we respond?" This well-know story could be given another name, "The man who took the opportunity to encounter God." The story initially presents a traveler who has encountered robbers, something we unfortunately hear about all too much in our contemporary world. The man is injured; he is unable to care for himself. The parable then presents three others who are given the opportunity to help, to befriend the injured man, to encounter God. The first two, the priest and the Levite, were highly respected members of the community, the kind of people society appreciates and in whom trust is placed. These two, one-by-one come upon the scene. They have the opportunity to help, but they do not take advantage of the opportunity afforded them. As St. Luke says, they simply passed by. The third man who comes upon the scene is a Samaritan. He was from the northern part of Israel. Samaria was the ancient land of the ten lost tribes conquered some 700 years before Jesus' birth. Jews did not trust Samaritans; they were never accepted in Hebrew society and not considered worthy of respect. Yet, this third man, the one who everyone hated and gave no chance, was the one who took the opportunity God gave to him to be neighbor to another.

God gives us many chances, many opportunities—do we use the opportunity, do we take advantage of the possibility, or do we merely pass by? The opportunity to be a neighbor, to show that we care and in the process show the face of God to others happens each day. Almost daily we encounter people who are hurt. It may be a person who hurts physically, like the man who fell among robbers. More often, however, we will find people who hurt inside, someone who has been wounded by the words and actions of others, events, or the cruelty of the world.

When someone hurts, when someone wants to talk, do we do as the priest and Levite and pass by or do we take the time and make the effort of the Samaritan and show God to others. We always cannot be there for others; there would be nothing left for ourselves. But what is our attitude? Is our heart open like the Samaritan or closed like the priest and Levite? Each one of us must answer this most challenging question! As the Book of Deuteronomy says, God's commandment to love is not mysterious or far off. "No, the word is very near to you; it is in your mouth and in your heart for you to observe." (30:14) We need only to carry it out!

As God presents chances for us, can we likewise open opportunities for others? St. Paul tells the Colossians that all are reconciled in Christ: "For in him all the fullness of God was pleased to dwell and through him God was pleased to reconcile to himself all things, whether on earth or in heaven, by making peace through the blood of his cross." (1:19-20) Are we reconciled with one another? Does everyone have an equal chance with us, or have some been written off as everyone wrote off Billy Mills? Have we written off individuals or groups as lazy, unproductive, or not useable? Have we said in essence, I don't need you; I will just pass you by?

This tendency can happen with all of us whatever our age may be. Children by ignoring their friends or refusing friendship say I don't need you; you are not my neighbor. Adults who continually refuse to respond to God's call found in the faces and voices of neighbors, the sick, the poor, the stranger say, I don't need you; you are not my neighbor. What an opportunity we miss. God is so near; we only need to open our eyes and see him!

God challenges us daily to be a neighbor to others. God opened a chance for Billy Mills who took it and won the gold medal. Likewise, we are given opportunities to find God, to be neighborly, and help others. Let us also take the opportunity and we too will gain eternal life, the most coveted of all gifts!

Question: Do I use wisely the opportunities God given me or do I simply pass them by?

Scripture Passage: "From everyone to whom much has been given, much will be required; and from the one to whom must has been entrusted, even more will be demanded." (Luke 12:48b)

Prayer: Jesus, open my eyes to your presence in every aspect of our world.

Allowing Jesus to Feed Us

Jimmy Harper wearily plodded home after a tough day on the job. As he walked he spied a bench alongside the road; he stopped and rested. As he waited, a women, hauling behind her a large cart of flowers, happened to pass by. The sweet smell of the flowers perfumed the air. Jimmy instantly lost the weariness in his body and his spirits were lifted as well. Never before had he experienced anything like this, especially from flowers, and he had many of them at his home. "How much are you asking for your flowers?" Jimmy asked the lady. "You may take as many as you wish," she replied. "There is no charge. Your gratitude and the proper use of the flowers is sufficient payment for me." Jimmy hurriedly gathered in his arms as many flowers as he could carry and, now renewed in body and spirit, continued his journey home.

When he arrived home and entered the front door, the sweet aroma of the flowers almost instantly permeated the house. Jimmy's wife and children came to the front room, realizing that something special was happening. They too had their weariness removed and their spirits lifted. In a very real way these flowers were feeding the Harper family.

Jimmy was concerned that the magic of the flowers be maintained. When the blossoms began to wither and die, he gathered them together and planted them is a small plot of land behind the house. With sunlight and water the flowers again bloomed and continued their magic. Never before had the Harper family had such solace from weariness, comfort from sorrow, and spiritual nourishment that these special flowers brought.

Jimmy was quite cautious about the flowers; he did not want anything to happen to them. At first his caution was seen only in a warning to his children, lest their energetic play result in trampling the flowers. Later, when the Harper children were more mature and guests were a regular occurrence at the house, Jimmy built a wall around the flowers to protect them. This caused much consternation in the family as now special permission was required and access was restricted to the flowers and to their special power. Later Jimmy found it necessary to hire a lawyer, judge and guards to adjudicate cases for access and to safeguard the flowers. In the process the family lost the special magic that the flowers had brought; they were no longer fed. In the end members of the Harper family, frustrated that the flowers were denied them, decided to seek the flower lady themselves. They searched the highways and byways; finally they found her. She was still giving away her flowers, free of charge, to any who would be grateful and would use them properly.[2]

Are you a person who lives to eat or one who eats to live? With respect to food, most of us, especially those who live in the so-called first world, would answer, we live to eat. Food is good and dining is pleasurable; it is a social norm. But for those who bear the name Christian, we must go one step further and ask this same question of our spiritual hunger. Do we live

---

[2] Paraphrased from "The Flower Lady," in John Aurelio, *Colors! Stories of the Kingdom* (New York: Crossroad, 1993), 146-47.

so as to be fed by that which God gives us, or do we merely eat, are we fed, simply to survive and get by. The story of Jimmy Harper and the flower lady challenges us to rethink our motivation about how we think of God and to remove barriers which hinder our preparation for Jesus.

God has always provided for all of us and what we receive allows us to do what is not humanly possible. Scripture provides several examples of this phenomenon. In I Kings (19:4-8) we encounter Elijah, the prophet of God, who like Jimmy Harper, is weary and afraid. He sits under a broom tree and asks for death. God's angel is sent to the prophet and he is told on two occasions to eat and drink. When he does this he is able to do what is not humanly possible; he walks forty days and forty nights to the mountain of God, Horeb. In the Bread of Life discourse in John's Gospel (Chapter 6) we read of how Jesus feeds us with bread, but the Lord provides so much more. Jesus gives us himself; he is the bread of the life. Those who receive this special gift are also able to do that which is not possible for humans; we inherit eternal life.

Jimmy Harper knew that the flowers were special and that they could perform wonders. But in his zeal to protect them he built barriers so high and strong between his family and the flowers that they could no longer work their magic. We many times also set up barriers which keep us from experiencing the presence of God. We place barriers before God's word. Sometimes we are lazy and other times we are too busy. Sometimes we just refuse to listen. We also place barriers between ourselves and others. We will only associate with certain groups of people, those who live in the same neighborhood, those who do the same line of work or those who have the same intellectual aptitude that we possess. Our attitudes cause us to miss many people and in the process we miss God as well.

St. Paul tells the Ephesians (4:31-32) that they are to rid themselves of malice, bitterness, and all other forms of vice and to replace them with an imitation of Christ. We can do this today by feeding ourselves on God's word, and the Christian community. Let us, therefore, open our hearts and minds, let us remove barriers which limit our preparedness for Jesus, the one who brings life today and eternal life forever.

Question: What barriers do I place, consciously or unconsciously between myself and God?

Scripture Passage: "In the wilderness prepare the way of the Lord, make straight in the desert a highway for our God." (Isaiah 40:3)

Prayer: God, help me to fill in the valleys and level off the mountains in building a highway to you.

Who Do You Say That I Am?

The time was the reconstruction period following the great American Civil War. The place was a small southern town. To that setting John Sommersby returned home, at least it seemed to be him. Everyone thought that Sommersby had died in the great war between the Union and the Confederacy; all the other soldiers had returned home some time before. He appeared to be different, but then people said that such a war changed a person in more than mind and spirit. He recognized his friends, however, and they recognized him; the whole town celebrated.

Still, despite the celebration there was some doubt as to the identity of the man who had returned. The family dog did not recognize him and pets never forget the scent of their masters. When Sommersby went to have a new pair of shoes made for himself the cobbler noticed that the pattern of his foot made before the war no longer fit. It would be Mrs. Sommersby, John's wife, however, who would be the critical judge. Was this rather gentle and kind man the same person who had gone to war six years previously, a man who had many times been harsh and cruel to her?

The town to which Sommersby returned had been devastated by the war. The Union army had plundered the city; economic ruin was a real possibility. A leader was necessary, one who could come forward to take charge and bring the town to greatness once again. That person would be John Sommersby. He had a plan to grow tobacco. Capital was necessary, however, for the initial investment of buying the precious and expensive tobacco seed. Confederate money was good no longer, thus the people brought what valuables the Yankees had not taken—rings, bracelets, a silver tea service and gave them to Sommersby to trade. They were ready to take the responsibility that such trust would entail.

Sommersby gathered the valuables and went to buy seed. Although it took longer than expected, he returned with the tobacco seed. The people planted the crop and nurtured it to maturity. The yield was great and the price per unit of measure was even greater than Sommersby himself thought possible. The town and its people would survive.

John Sommersby, however, would not be able to taste the sweetness of victory. Accused of wrong doing during the war he was tried and convicted. His punishment was to be hanged until dead. But was this man John Sommersby or someone who looked a great deal like him. The world would never know. The people in Sommersby's town had placed their trust in him, taken responsibility and tasted victory. John Sommersby, or whoever this man was, demonstrated his loyalty to those who trusted him.

"Who do you say that I am?" The great question which Jesus asks his apostles (Matthew 16:15) is answered in a romantic way in the motion picture Sommersby. It is answered in a true and pragmatic way by Jesus himself. Jesus poses the initial question, "Who do people say that the Son of Man is?" The response comes from the disciples, "Some say John the Baptist, but others Elijah, and still others Jeremiah or one of the prophets." Jesus is not satisfied with this response; he probes deeper. "But who do you say that I am?" (Matthew 16:13b,15a) Peter steps forward to answer. Peter is the one who the Synoptic Evangelists many times portray as the apostle who never quite understands. Peter is the one who will later deny the Lord three times on the night before he died. But this is Peter's hour of glory for he says, "You are the Messiah, the Son of the living God." (16:16)

Jesus is pleased with Peter's response. Peter will be the rock upon which the Church will be built; he will be given a privileged position. But with the position comes responsibility. Peter will be given the keys of the Kingdom. For Peter and for all those who have followed him in professing Jesus as Lord, the responsibility of pasturing the sheep, the people of God, is great.

What happens if we refuse to carry out the responsibilities that our position asks of us? The Prophet Isaiah (22:15-23) provides us an answer by telling us about Shebna, a royal official who was master of the palace. With such an exalted position came responsibility, but Shebna failed to carry out his duties. Thus God will thrust him down from his elevated position. Both position and responsibility will be given to Eliakim. The moral of the story is clear: properly exercise the responsibility given because of your position or lose the position and the responsibility forever.

Jesus' question hits us as they say "right between the eyes": "Who do you say that I am?" If Jesus was not important, if his message had no relevance for us then we would have no responsibility; we would have no privileges either. If the Mystical Body, the community of the Church, had no significance for us then again we would have no responsibility to one another or to God. But the fact is that there is not one person who bears the name Christian in this category, for whether it was many years ago or just yesterday we have all declared that Jesus is Lord. Our profession of faith requires us to be responsible people. The people in John Sommersby's town placed their trust in him and took their responsibility. Peter professed faith in Jesus and led the Church through those very difficult early years after the Lord's ascension. What about all of us?

Youth need to bring Jesus to the situation in which they find themselves. Bring Christ to the classroom; bring Christ to the athletic field; bring the Lord to social situations and events. Bring Christ to your relationships with family and friends. Refuse to give into the ideas of society which promote violence and other forms of behavior that lead one away from Christ. Do your best to promote the message of Jesus, one of peace, justice, and compassion.

Working people and parents have a special and unique responsibility as well. They say that the work place is a jungle and it probably is. The jungle promotes an unchristian work ethic. Refuse to give into such pressure; rather find alternate ways of doing the job, ways that are in line with the teachings of Jesus. Parents have the most difficult task in the world. Do not take the responsibility of being Christian parents lightly. Be parents as Christ would have you be. Jesus gathered the children around him; he asked us to have the attitude of children.

People whose children are grown and those who are retired have a significant responsibility. Possibly the greatest contribution you can make is to use the extra time that you might have wisely. Retired people can use their time, expertise, and resources for the betterment of all, as a means of exercising their Christian responsibility.

Jesus' question continues to stand before us, "Who do you say that I am?" We have been baptized in the waters of salvation; we have been fully initiated in the Church and can unhesitatingly profess that Jesus is Lord. This profession of faith gives us the privilege of being children of God; it also asks something of us. Let us never be sidetracked from this most important of all responsibilities. Let us also remember that we do not walk the Christian road alone. We have the one person we need for as Jesus says at the end of St. Matthew's Gospel (28:19-20): "Go therefore and make disciples of all nations, baptizing them in the name of the Father and of the Son and of the Holy Spirit and teaching them to obey everything that I have commanded you. And remember I am with you always to the end of the age."

Question: Do I willingly engage my Christian responsibilities or am I less diligent than I need to be?

Scripture Passage: "If you confess with your lips that Jesus is Lord and believe in your heart that God raised him from the dead, you will be saved." (Romans 10:9)

Prayer: Lord, help me to be responsible to my family, friends and the tasks you give me.

The Challenge of Tough Love

The time was November 1930. The place was the Memorial Coliseum in Los Angeles, California. The event was the annual gridiron clash between college football powerhouses, Notre Dame and the University of Southern California (USC). On one side of the field, decorated in cardinal and gold, stood Howard Jones, the successful and well-respected football coach at USC. On the visitor's side of the field stood Knute Rockne, arguably the most famous football coach of all time. The experts, the oddsmakers, had predicted that the game would not be close; they favored USC by 15 points.

That year Notre Dame used its famous "box" formation, a version of the old single-wing offense. Frank Corridio, the Irish quarterback, had been a star that season and had earned the honored distinction of "All American." Corridio, however, would not be a major factor in the game. The stars would be two rather unheralded players—Bucky O'Connor, a third-team halfback, who played only because of injuries to teammates, and Hal "Watch-dial" Metzger, a 165-pound running guard.

The opening play from scrimmage forecast the afternoon's events. O'Connor took a handoff and behind the blocking of Metzger, who would knocked down one man, then a brush blocked a second and then a third defender, ran 80 yards for a touchdown. Notre Dame never looked back. When the dust had cleared, the spikes had been hung up, and all the fans had gone home, the scoreboard read, Notre Dame—27, USC—0. The Irish had scored a great victory, an upset. Yet, Notre Dame lost something much greater that day; Knute Rockne had coached his last game. He died the next spring on March 31 in an infamous plane crash.

Knute Rockne was a coach; he was a friend. Above all he was a man who loved. Rockne was successful, the most successful football coach in Notre Dame history. Why was he successful? Certainly he had great players. Rockne coached some of the best players of the day, many of whom, like Frank Corridio, earned the coveted title of "All American." Rockne was successful, however, because he was a man who had learned to love and, thereby, to teach responsibility.

Rockne was often quoted, "People call me a roughneck." In many ways that is exactly what he was. He was strict with his players. He expected them to be in the best mental and physical condition that they could attain. Moreover, however, Rockne taught his players that football was a team game that was won when players cared for and took responsibility for each other.

At another time Rockne said, "Football teaches responsibility." There is a certain interconnectedness to the game. A third-team halfback and a 165-pound running guard demonstrated such a connectedness that November afternoon in Los Angeles. Rockne demanded a lot from his players. If there was something wrong, he would tell them about it. His direction, his method of coaching, was in a very real way a form of love, a love which taught responsibility, first to self and most especially for others.

Scripture speaks of our need to take responsibility for others as the one debt of love which we owe to all. The prophet Ezekiel tells us that we must take the responsibility necessary to challenge others. We read, "So you, mortal, I have made a sentinel for the house of Israel; whenever you hear a word from my mouth, you shall give them warning from me." (33:7). In other words if we see an individual in error, we must take the time to correct that person. Equally we could say that if we see someone in a more general need we must aid that person. God also says through Ezekiel, "If I say to the wicked, 'O wicked ones, you shall surely die,' and you do not speak to warn the wicked to turn from their ways, the wicked shall die in their iniquity, but their blood I will require at your hand." (33:8). If we refuse to aid another, if we will not take the time to correct someone who is in error, then we will be held accountable for our failure to act.

In Matthew's Gospel, Jesus also speaks of our responsibility for others. We read, "If another member of the church sins against you, go and point out the fault when the two of you can be alone." (18:15). Today we call Jesus' challenge fraternal correction. Jesus challenges us and we must not fail to act; we must do what is necessary. The Lord also says that we must be decisive in what we do. As we read, "Truly I tell you, whatever you bind on earth will be bound in heaven, and whatever you loose on earth will be loosed in heaven." (Matthew 18:18)

Fraternal correction and challenging others, when done properly and with the correct attitude, are true acts of love. They are not acts of love that are easily visible, but they are, nonetheless absolutely essential. It is this same love of which St. Paul speaks when he writes to the Christian community at Rome: "Owe no one anything, except to love one another; for the one who loves another has fulfilled the law." (Romans 13:8) In other words, if we have loved we have paid our debt; we need do nothing more.

Learning to love is a great challenge. Some forms of love, such as the Greek concept of *eros* or romantic love, come quite naturally. Certainly romantic love takes work; it is not easy. But *eros* is generated by feelings of the heart; it does not come from the brain. Love can and must be deeper and more broad than our feelings alone. Love means being honest. This might mean for each of us that we need to separate ourselves from an individual, a situation or a movement which gets us nowhere, at least nowhere that we need or want to be. Honesty might also mean having the courage to challenge someone who we love very much and tell that person that there is a problem that needs to be corrected.

Tough love is the ability to love when it is most difficult. Tough love is when we refuse to accept the excuses of the addict and suggest treatment or counseling. Tough love is challenging a young person whose relationships or behavior are problematic or destructive. Tough love at work means drawing the line and refusing to participate in unethical work practices and challenging others to follow your lead.

Love truly is responsibility; love is challenge. It is not easy to challenge others, to be confrontative, especially in a society which tells us to mind our own business and not get involved. Yet, Scripture tells us that we must be responsible to others, as the only debt of love that we owe. Let us realize that love is much more than flowers sent, kinds words spoken, and signs of affection. Knute Rockne showed love as a coach and through that action taught responsibility. In the process he earned a permanent place in the history of sports. Let us also know that we too must show love and demonstrate it by being responsible, so that we can also earn a permanent place, in eternity with God.

Question: Can I be more responsible and exercise tough love when acquiescence is easier?

Scripture Passage: "Owe no one anything, except to love one another; for the one who loves another has fulfilled the law." (Romans 13:8)

Prayer: Lord, strengthen my resolve to love in the most trying circumstances.

Reconciliation: The Journey of Faith

Life is a journey, which like all journeys, has a beginning, a middle, and an end. Birth is the beginning of our journey and the day-to-day events of our life are its great middle. Death signals the end of the journey of life. Within the journey of life there are numerous shorter or sub journeys, each of which has a beginning, a middle, and an end. There is the journey of youth which begins with birth, continues with the primary and secondary school years, and closes with graduation, entrance into college or the first major job. There is the journey of one's occupation which begins with one's first full time employment, continues with the peaks and valleys of the working world, and ends with retirement after many years. There is the journey of adulthood which for most begins when we move away from home, continues in our chosen vocation of work and lifestyle, and ends with our death.

One journey within the journey of life which accompanies us along the road is our life of faith. Faith has a beginning, at least in a formal sense, through baptism. The long middle ground of faith is our life, the numerous times we encounter God and find ecstasy and the times when we fail to see or even shut out God. The journey of faith, like the journey of life has ups and downs. The journey of faith has an end as well, the day of our judgment by God. This special journey runs parallel with another journey without which faith makes little sense—the journey of reconciliation.

The journey of reconciliation is a process by which Christians are reunited with God and God's people. Since reconciliation is a process it possesses certain elements than can be identified. Each element is essential to the unity of the whole; they feed off one another. If we cannot achieve the first step, then those that follow may not be attainable.

The first element is passive but absolutely essential to the process. We need to believe that God never gives up on us. The story in Luke's Gospel (13:6-9) about the barren fig tree demonstrates God's ever present love. The tree representing Israel has not been fruitful. The owner wants it cut down but the vinedresser says to give it another chance. The second, the third, the hundredth chance is always ours with the ever-present mercy of God. When we know that God never gives up, that God pursues us, as described in Francis Thompson's poem "The Hound of Heaven," then we know that reconciliation has begun.

The process of reconciliation continues with the discovery of the three active aspects of forgiveness, within self, with others, and ultimately with God. The famous parable of The Prodigal Son, Luke 15:11-32, best illustrates this second step in the journey of reconciliation. Active reconciliation must begin within our own person. The so-called prodigal son in the story comes to the realization that he needs to forgive himself. He has wasted his father's money; he has lived a wayward existence. Before he could begin the physical journey back to his father he needed to find a change of heart within himself. He needed to forgive himself, before he would be ready to accept the forgiveness of others.

Reconciliation with others is the second active aspect. The older son in the parable is representative of one who cannot forgive others. He is angry with his brother for his wayward actions. He is even more incensed, however, by his father who has not only forgiven the younger boy's transgressions but has celebrated his return with food and dance. We learn about the need to forgive others "through the back door" in the character of the older son. Since this young man cannot forgive, the process of reconciliation is stunted. As when the weak link in the chain snaps and destroys the usefulness of the whole, so too if either of the first two active aspects of reconciliation are not found, the final aspect, reconciliation with God, cannot be achieved.

The forgiving father in the parable represents God. His youngest son was barely in sight and the father had the celebration prepared. Reconciliation was achieved as soon as his wayward son realized that he needed to be forgiven, by himself and by others. Jesus' arms are outstretched on the Cross as a sign of his welcome of us when we have strayed off the path that leads to life. All that is necessary to achieve this reconciliation is for us to ask.

The final step in the process of reconciliation might not seem obvious. God has pursued us and we have found reconciliation within ourselves, with others and with God. One thing more is required, however; we need to look to the future. The positive message of the prophets is to look to the future. After predictions of doom the prophets say that the people need to forget the past and look to the future. Isaiah writes, "Do not remember the former things or consider the things of old. I am about to do a new thing; now it springs forth, do you not perceive it? I will make a way in the wilderness and rivers in the desert." (43:18-19). The past actions of the Hebrew people had to be put behind them; they needed to begin anew.

Reconciliation is only complete when we put the sins of our past behind us and start again. If we dwell on the past then it will be impossible to make a new beginning. We carry around our excess baggage; it weighs us down. But as Jesus said to the women caught in adultery, "'Woman, where are they? Has no one condemned you?' She said, 'No one, sir.' And Jesus said, 'Neither do I condemn you. Go your way, and from now on do not sin again.'" (John 8:10b-11). Jesus' words to the woman point to the future. The past is forgiven. Let us move on, drop the past baggage, and try to do better. Too many times people live in the past; they have never learned to forgive themselves.

Reconciliation is very much a desert experience. When we don't feel right in our relationships with ourselves, others, and God, then we feel we are apart from our heart's desire, distanced from the world, alone in the desert. But when reconciliation is achieved, when the process is completed, then we feel again like members of the community.

The journey of faith includes many aspects including the process of reconciliation. The process of being reconciled begins passively with God's pursuit of us, moves active with forgiveness within self, others, and God, and concludes with a look to the future. God is waiting for us; the rest is up to us. Let us center our thoughts on what could be; think of the water in the desert for which we long, and strive to find new waters of life today and each day of our lives.

Question: Am I judgmental in my attitudes toward others or do I seek the spirit of reconciliation?

Scripture Passage: "Lord, if another member of the church sins against me, how often should I forgive? As many as seven times? Jesus said, 'Not seven times, but, I tell you, seventy-seven times.'" (Luke 18:21-22)

Prayer: Lord, help me to forgive and be forgiven.

Stewards of God's Gifts

About thirty miles north of San Francisco, west of Interstate 101, nestled in a quiet and serene valley, you will find Muir Woods. In this place of beauty and tranquility one can still see nature untouched by human hands. Majestic redwoods grow straight and tall reaching heights many times greater than 200 feet. A beautiful stream runs through the park; wild animals including deer and many species of birds are present. The scene at Muir Woods is nature as God gave it to us.

John Muir, the man whose name graces this patch of untouched nature, was a naturalist, but his career was not always one of conservation; he had to learn. Born in Scotland in the mid-nineteenth century, Muir emigrated to the United States as a young man. He was truly the stereotypical man of the world. He was an inventor of mechanical devices. His philosophy was that the world should be used for one's personal advancement and merit.

In 1867, however, Muir experienced conversion in his attitude toward life. That year while working in his laboratory an accident almost cost him his sight. The experience caused Muir to reevaluate his life and change direction. He traveled from the East and eventually reached California. There he discovered the Yosemite Valley and Sequoia Forest. After surveying the land for several years, Muir in 1876 asked Congress to adopt a forest conservation program. He believed that the beauty and resources of the land should be appreciated and used by all, not by individuals for personal gain. Muir fought against those who wished to exploit the land for personal profit. In the end John Muir's efforts to conserve the natural wonders of the land were successful. We can see the fruits of his efforts in the national park system which was inaugurated in the first years of the twentieth century by President Theodore Roosevelt.

The legacy of John Muir is one of stewardship, the ability to properly use God's gifts. In Scripture we hear this same message, one might say "through the back door," by examples of improper use of God's gifts. In the parable of the corrupt manager (Luke 16:1-13) we hear that the manager was not a good steward; he tried to steal from others. Today we would say he was "ripping them off." The owner, however, caught his manager in his theft; he would need to change. The manager's solution to the dilemma was quite unique. He is given credit for his shrewdness, for his initiative. We must see, however, that the manager is not praised for his misuse of resources, only his ability to find solutions. Jesus' warning in the Gospel is straight forward—you cannot give yourself to God and money. In other words you cannot be selfish with God's gifts. We must use God's gifts, the resources of this world, prudently. We must be faithful servants of God's gifts to all.

Faithful stewardship has been and continues to be a problem in our world. The prophet Amos (8:4-6) speaks against the injustice of the rich: "Hear this, you that trample on the needy, and bring to ruin the poor of the land, saying 'when will the new moon be over so we may sell grain; and the Sabbath so we may offer wheat for sale? We will make the ephah small and the shekel great, and practice deceit with false balances, buying the poor for silver and the needy for a pair of sandals, and selling the sweepings of the wheat."

The problem of which Amos speaks and Jesus gives warning is still with us in contemporary society. Unfair practices, in work and society in general, are common in our world. We all know that the rich are getting richer and poor are becoming poorer; the middle class is shrinking. Why is this happening? One reason certainly must be that people are greedy. People want more and more; they use the world's resources for personal gain alone. Such people have never become good stewards of God's gifts. In our world a few people have much, while most have little. Sociologists speak about the north-south split in the world's continents. In the North live those who have much; in the South live those who possess little. This is easy to see by contrasting those who live in Europe and North America with those who live in South America and Africa. But let us not forget that this split in rich and poor exists is our own backyard, the inner cities of our own country.

Our Christian call to stewardship needs to begin with the right attitude. We must realize that the world's goods are for all. If we always put ourselves first, if we think only of our own needs, then we cannot be good stewards. Thinking only of self fails to see that we are a world community, we are all brothers and sisters in Christ. If we are not careful we will wind up "ripping people off," maybe not materially, but more importantly in our attitudes which keep people down and unable to raise themselves to the proper level of dignity which is theirs.

Like the initiative shown by the clever manager in the aforementioned parable, we must use the gifts of God for the benefit of all. We must be prudent; we must put God and God's people before personal profit and gain. God's gifts serve all. It may be the gift of nature, as John Muir saw it; it may be the gifts of the world. Let our attitude and action today show that we too can be good stewards, sharing in God's love for all people.

Question: Do I use well and properly the things of the world or do I abuse them?

Scripture Passage: "This is my commandment, that you love one another as I have loved you." (John 15:12)

Prayer: Lord, make me a good steward of your manifold gifts.

Our Commitment to the Lord

"Old soldiers never die, they just fade away. And like the old soldier of that ballad, I too will just fade away." These famous words were spoken by General Douglas MacArthur in his farewell speech to Congress April 19, 1951. This speech was delivered after an illustrious career of over forty years of military service. General MacArthur's words were a message of his faithfulness to duty, honor, and country, the West Point motto upon which he based his service and life.

The career of Douglas MacArthur was an expression of the words he used in his farewell speech. What he did was important, but his faithfulness to commitment and purpose made his career significant. MacArthur served his country in three different wars. He was a general in charge of a tank company in the European theater during World War I. During the Second World War he was Allied Commander in the Pacific theater. His famous words upon abandoning the Philippine Islands in the face of the Japanese onslaught, "I shall return," were immortalized in 1944 when Allied forces returned to that besieged country to reclaim the land. After the War, MacArthur was made commander of United States occupation forces in Japan. After two wars and thirty-five years service one might think of retirement, but not Douglas MacArthur. When the Korean conflict began in 1950 MacArthur was again called upon to serve. As United Nations Commander in 1951-1952 the General again demonstrated his faithfulness; he truly believed in "Duty, Honor, Country." It was not, however, his work or accomplishments that ultimately mattered, but rather his belief in principle and commitment.

The life of Douglas MacArthur, as an example, well illustrates one of the central messages of Sacred Scripture—the human call to service, commitment to duty, and ultimately a call to faith. St. Luke (17:5-10) describes Jesus' rather unusual response when the apostles demand "Increase our faith!" Jesus' words sound rather harsh: "Who among you would say to your slave who has just come in from plowing or tending sheep in the field, 'Come here at once and take your place at table?' Would you not rather say to him, 'Prepare supper for me, put on your apron and serve me while I eat and drink; later you may eat and drink?'" (17:7-8) He goes on to say that, we are useless servants, we are only doing our duty. The Gospel seems to indicate that service is an expectation. For we who profess the name Christian, God's call to ministry is an expectation. Through baptism we have all been called to faith and service. It is that mustard seed of faith inside each one of us, which the Gospel describes, that allows our work, our service, to have meaning.

With faith all our work, all that we do, is ultimately God's work. Jesus is not physically present with us; thus we become the hands, the feet, the eyes of God. We need not be congratulated for what we do. The reward for the just person with faith is life now, and in the end eternal life with God. Certainly one can expect nothing greater.

The book of Habakkuk, one of the minor and lesser known prophets, exhorts us to duty and service. The prophet, in conversation with God, makes a plea for justice. Why doesn't God listen; why does violence exist? Why is there misery all around? God's response, like Jesus' words in Luke's Gospel, is a bit confusing. God says not to be rash and not to rush. Have faith and do your duty; this is what God expects. In short Habakkuk and Jesus say the same thing. It is not what you ultimately do that counts. Rather what is important is the attitude one takes in what one does. Are we servants of the Lord; are we doing our duty? Are we, through faith, committed to God's work?

Few of us will ever live a life where commitment to ideals and principles is as obvious and public as it was for Douglas MacArthur. Nevertheless, we all are called to live the commitment of our baptism, through ministry, service and love. We need to demonstrate commitment to family and friends. This will require channeling our energy towards a commitment of time and effort in the betterment of others. It will be mean a commitment of our resources, monies and material possessions towards the things of community and not personal gain alone. Commitment is also required in our place of work. We need to be faithful in our presence, to give an honest day's labor and to complete our assigned tasks as best we can. Ultimately we must be committed to God. We need to spend time with God each day in prayer. We need to be faithful to our sacramental life, through the Eucharist and reconciliation. Our commitment to God is manifest through our works of charity and peace as well, especially for those who have most need of our assistance. Today let us renew our commitment to self, to others, and to God. Let us be reminded of our duty. Let us seek no compensation, except the reward of eternal life with God. For our purposes today possibly we can change the words of General MacArthur and apply them to ourselves: Old Christians do die, they don't just fade away, but like the Christians of that ballad, Christians of commitment, they die unto eternal life.

Question: What level of commitment do I demonstrate toward the varied responsibilities of my life?

Scripture Passage: "When you have done all that you were ordered to do, say, 'We are worthless slaves; we have done only what we ought to have done.'"(Luke 17:10)

Prayer: Lord, help me to be committed to you and all God's people.

Welcoming God in One Another

Harriet Tubman was born into slavery in Dorchester County Maryland in 1821. Like all slaves in that period Harriet, together with her ten siblings and parents worked the fields, in this case a large tobacco plantation. Day after day, week by week over many years, slaves did the same thing. At sunrise work began and at sundown it ended; the monotony of daily life was severe. Certainly slavery was an ignoble existence, not only because of the menial and back-breaking work, but more importantly because it was a life which degraded human dignity. Slaves were not only perceived as unimportant humans, they were considered non-persons. Harriet Tubman never received a word of encouragement, welcome, or invitation in her early life, either from her white slave master or her fellow black slaves, who had been beaten down so severely by life that they no longer possessed any self respect.

This was the life of Harriet in her early days, but in 1849 she managed to escape to the North and freedom. These were the high days of the American abolition movement, led by the Irish nationalist, William Lloyd Garrison. Harriet quickly joined this movement and soon thereafter became a "conductor" on what was known as the underground railroad—a secret organization which smuggled slaves to freedom in the North. In the ten years prior to the commencement of the Civil War Harriet Tubman made at least fifteen expeditions into the southern regions of Maryland and in the process rescued over two hundred slaves. She continued her work even when a large reward was put forward for her capture and arrest. Harriet Tubman had never been given a word of kindness, welcome, or invitation in her days as a slave, but her life as a "conductor" with the underground railroad exemplified these important qualities. Slaves called her Moses, not only because she was their deliverer, but more importantly because she cared about them. John Brown, whose failed raid at Harper's Ferry focused national attention on the issue of slavery, called her General Tubman. Harriet Tubman gave welcome to all she found in distress and invited them to ride with her to freedom. In a similar way, we are challenged to give welcome to God by welcoming one another.

In the Book of Genesis (18:1-10) Abraham encounters three men. He has no idea who these people are—they may be criminals, murderers, or thieves, or they may be messengers of God. Who they are is not important to Abraham; what they are, namely strangers in need of hospitality, means everything. Abraham and his wife Sarah immediately drop what they are doing and see to their duties of hospitality. They prepare a meal; they welcome the strangers into their home. Because of the couple's loving presence and attitude, the strangers say that they will return in one year and Sarah will have a son. The great promise of progeny for which Abraham and Sarah had waited will be their's.

The Lukan account of Jesus' visit to the home of Martha and Mary (10:38-42) contrasts two ways of demonstrating welcome. Most all people can relate to Martha's request of Jesus, "Lord… tell her to help me." She has worked hard to prepare for Jesus' arrival and she wants some assistance and recognition for her efforts. Like Martha most of us, more than once, have done all the work of hospitality, received little recognition, and have felt disappointed when no one seemed to care. It is important to understand that Jesus in not critical of what Martha has done.

On the contrary, the work of hospitality is very important. But Jesus uses this event, as he does all such opportunities, to teach. The lesson is clear—as important as is the work of hospitality to the individual, there is something more valuable, the need to give welcome to God. Mary, by placing herself at the feet of the Lord and listening to his words, welcomed God. As Jesus says, "Mary has chosen the better part which will not be taken away from her." (10:42b)

We have all been called to bring welcome and invitation to God by showing hospitality to all we meet. We know that God is not visible in our world, but the living presence of God abides in each one of us. Remember that Genesis says that we are all made in the image and likeness of God. We, therefore, are the presence of God to others—such an awesome responsibility. We must do God's work; we must build the Kingdom. We must bid welcome to all who come to us, both those we know and maybe more especially those who are strangers. It is not easy to bid welcome to all, but then Christianity, when lived properly, is a great challenge. Some people are difficult to deal with and others we shun intentionally. We make people strangers and aliens by how we treat them. When we disregard others merely because they are too old, are of a different ethnic heritage, speak a different language, possess other ideas or practice different customs, we have failed in our obligation to bid welcome to all.

I am certain that Harriet Tubman never consciously thought that her work as a "conductor" on the underground railroad was the action of welcoming God, but her life clearly demonstrates how she fulfilled the great challenge which Scripture places before us. Let us bid welcome and show we care to all we meet. The author of the Letter to the Hebrews (13:2) has summarized our responsibility: "Do not neglect to show hospitality to strangers, for by doing that some have entertained angels without knowing it."

Question: Do people find welcome in my attitude, actions and words of do they receive another message?

Scripture Passage: "In that renewal there is no longer Greek and Jew, circumcised and uncircumcised, barbarian, Scythian, slave and free; but Christ is all in all." (Colossians 3:11)

Prayer: Lord Jesus, may I welcome you by welcoming my sisters and brothers.

An Agent of Salvation

Giacomo Nerone first appeared in the village of Gemello Minore sometime during the war. He had been wounded in a local skirmish, but exactly how he arrived in the village was a mystery. A little investigation revealed that Giacomo had deserted his unit and was, therefore, a fugitive. Giacomo Nerone was a difficult man as well; he did not play by all the rules. Yet, there was something about this man which was attractive to others. He was the type of person who grows on you.

Despite his charm, Giacomo was known to be a sinful man; he was far from perfect. While he was in the village he fathered a bastard son. He was often argumentative and pushy. Because he had deserted his unit, the people in the village could not trust him with even small tasks. The reality of his brokenness was experienced by all in the village.

Despite his sinfulness, Giacomo had a profoundly positive influence on many in the village. He was able to transform the earthy and quite worldly Padre Anselmo to a better understanding of his role as priest and minister to God's people. He befriended the irascible and hated Jewish doctor Aldo Meyer and made him feel welcome. He brought the face of God to the Countess di Sanctis, a woman who all others in the village had rejected. In short, Giacomo Nerone brought faith and hope to people who many times lived in despair and fear.

The paradoxical nature of his life would end with his death. He was executed by those in the village who saw him as a sinner and criminal. Now fifteen years later, the same people who asked for his life were proclaiming the sanctity of Giacomo Nerone. He was not perfect, but he possessed a goodness rarely seen or shared. He did not follow all of the rules, but he had special qualities that all wanted. While some sat around and allowed others to lead, and still others jockeyed for position in the realm of temporal status, Giacomo quietly and quite unassumingly, brought the face of God to others.

Was Giacomo Nerone a saint of a sinner? It was the task of Monsignor Blaise Meredith, an American priest sent by the Holy See, to investigate, question, and ultimately to determine who this man was. In the end, this cleric of little emotion discovered for himself what it truly means to be an agent of God's salvation to others.

The Devil's Advocate, one of the early and still popular novels of Morris West, challenges our sensibilities as to what is necessary for salvation. Scripture asks the same question, what is ultimately necessary for salvation? By looking at various models of human understanding and action, and with the perfect example of God, we can come to some answers to this great question.

The Prophet Ezekiel (34:11-17) presents us with both a passive model of human action and the perfect example of God as the Good Shepherd. Ezekiel analogizes humans to sheep who passively allow God to control their lives. The Good Shepherd goes after those who stray away, binds up those who are ill, and rescues those who are scattered. God gives us the perfect example of how to lead our lives. It is the action of God which gives us positive direction in our life.

St. Paul in I Corinthians 15:20-28 gives us a more active model of human action—we hear of the human desire for position. Paul describes Jesus as the one who destroys sovereignty, authority, and power. Position, in other words, has no importance in the eyes of God. Position gets us nowhere that we need or want to be.

St. Matthew's description of the Last Judgment (25:31-46) presents another active model, the idea of being a servant. In his eschatological discourse, Jesus tells us what is important, what truly makes a difference in our lives. Those who take the time, those who give food and drink, those who bind up the injured, those who visit the sick and the imprisoned, those, in other words, who treat others with love and compassion, will receive the reward of the eternal presence of God. Those, on the other hand, who refuse to take the time, those who show no love or compassion, especially to one of the least of our brothers and sisters, will lose the presence of God forever.

The Word of God tells us that what ultimately matters in our life is how we treat each other, how we show the face of God to our sisters and brothers. We must be agents of God's salvation to others. We may be leaders of followers. If we choose to be passive and allow others to lead, or if we have the gifts and talents to lead and choose to do so, we are not in any way leading lives that take us away from God. Scripture presents many actions that have the possibility for goodness and, therefore, holiness. However, what separates the sheep from the goats, the redeemed from the condemned, is our ability to be servants, live for others, and act as agents of God's salvation.

We all must take stock of our role in God's plan. Each of us has a role. It is unique, different, and special for each person. With some people our roles will intersect and mesh well; with others they will probably clash. Some will find peace in being passive and allowing God to control things. Others, who are gifted as leaders, will participate in the necessary task of temporal leadership. But, all of us must take the time, we must make the effort to do what is necessary to be agents of God's salvation to others. As the second half of the Golden Rule says we must love others as we love ourselves.

Giacomo Nerone was not perfect; he did not follow all the rules. Yet, the people of Gemello Minore proclaimed his sanctity because he took the time and through his efforts many were led to see the face of God. In the end Blaise Meredith, the Devil's Advocate, would discover this reality. Let us, therefore, reflect in our lives on our common vocation to be servants, agents of God's salvation. Let us hope and pray that if we were ever placed on trial for being God's agents there would be sufficient evidence to convict us. The sentence we will receive is eternal life.

Question: What priority do I place on serving others in our world?

Scripture Passage: "The greatest among you will be your servant." (Matthew 23:11)

Prayer: Father in heaven, make me of your peace.

Discovering God's Will

When Charlie Atlas was a teenager his parents bought him a dresser mirror that he placed in his bedroom. Before this time whenever Charlie needed to use a mirror he went to the bathroom, but there he was only able to see his head and possibly his shoulders. When he got dressed up for church or a date he used his parents' full length mirror in their bedroom. Charlie was happy with his new mirror; he spent many hours in front of it.

One day when he was standing in front of the mirror, Charlie decided to take off his shirt. He was very disappointed. His chest was scrawny and his biceps were so thin that he could place his hand completely around one. This was an intolerable situation; he did not want to be known as a scrawny weakling. Thus, on that very day Charlie Atlas made a pact with himself; he would work as hard as necessary in order to build up his upper body, so that he would not be embarrassed in the mirror ever again. Charlie began a rugged daily regimen of exercise. For several hours each and every day he did exercises—push-ups, pull-ups and sit-ups. Later he began to lift weights—barbells and dumbbells. He bought a special machine with weights, pulleys, and springs which allowed him to exercise even more.

After several months Charlie again looked in the mirror. There was definite improvement. His chest had grown and his arms were more muscular. The positive results encouraged him and, thus, he doubled his efforts. He did more difficult exercises, lifted heavier weights, and now even began to eat only certain foods. He took lots of vitamins as well. After a few years of this strenuous exercise program Charlie again looked in the mirror. He was quite satisfied, even elated. His chest was huge and taut and his biceps were so large that two hands could not encircle one. His stomach rippled like waves on the ocean. As he stood in personal admiration, all of a sudden Charlie collapsed. His parents were quite concerned and rushed him to the doctor. They thought for certain that it was a case of over exertion, but the doctor after examining Charlie said it was much more simple. Charlie's ankles and legs were too weak, they could not support his massive bulk, thus he collapsed. You see Charlie could only see his upper body in the mirror and that was all he developed.[3]

In different ways we are all like Charlie Atlas. Few people spend the time he spent in building our bodies, but we do spend lots of time working on the externals in our lives, our physical condition, our mind, our appearance. We live in the here and now and concern ourselves with that which is present before us. But like Charlie Atlas, as well, we fail many times to build up the foundation, that which is most basic in our lives and gives support to the externals that others see. For humans the foundation is our heart.

In Mark's Gospel (7:1-23) Jesus chastises the Scribes and Pharisees because they spend so much time working on the externals, the outside things in life. These Jewish religious leaders were all caught up in ritual purity and the civil law. Jesus tells them, "You abandon the commandment of God and

---

[3] Paraphrased from "Charlie Atlas and the Dresser Mirror," in John Aurelio, *Colors! Stories of the Kingdom* (New York: Crossroad, 1993), 26-27.

hold to human tradition." (7:8) Quoting the prophet Isaiah, He excoriates their misplaced priorities: "This people honors me with their lips, but their heads are far from me; in vain do they worship me, teaching human precepts as doctrines." (7:6b-7) The Scribes and Pharisees have failed to recognize the need for God in their hearts; they have forgotten what is most basic to them. The fruits of their failure can be seen. Those who fail to develop their hearts take the good gifts which God gives and somehow within themselves abuse them so that the results are greed, envy, murder, adultery, theft, and other such vices and sins.

We need to develop our hearts and we have been given the tools to do it. St. James (1:17) states, "Every generous act of giving, with every perfect gift, is from above, coming down from the Father of lights, with whom there is no variation or shadow due to change." Moreover, James says that the word of God has been planted down deep inside each one of us, in our hearts. It is this word that can lead us to salvation. But we must act on this word. If we merely listen and fail to act then we deceive ourselves (1:21-22). The gifts we have been given will become stagnant; they will not bear fruit.

Have we developed our externals alone or have we been developing our hearts as well? One way to get at this question is to ask a second proposition. Why do we do what we do; what is our motivation? Do we do the things we do out of a sense of duty alone? The birthday gift, the wedding ceremony, the company social gathering—do we do what we do because we are supposed to or because we want to do it? Have we been developing the affective, the heart side, so that all that we do, even our sense of duty, is done with a strong spiritual base and foundation?

How do we develop our hearts? The first thing we must realize is that such a task does not happen overnight. Like the development of our minds or our bodies, it takes lots of time and effort to build up our hearts. Charlie Atlas spent much time each day in building his upper body; we too must spend time each day in the development of our hearts, that is our relationship with God. We must take time in prayer, speaking with God and listening to God. We must spend time in reflection and meditation upon God's word so that we can listen to God's message and in that silence "hear" what God asks of us. We need to spend time with God. Maybe we can afford only one day away from what we normally do; maybe we can attend a weekend retreat. Possibly we are fortunate enough to be able to spend seven or more days in quiet solitude with God.

We can build up the outside, the externals which all can see and experience, but unless we build up the heart, our foundational relationship with God, then all will go to waste. Charlie Atlas built his upper body to a state of near perfection, but because he failed to build his foundation all was ruined. We have all heard the expression, "I am all dressed up and no where to go." This is the same idea—unless we build up the base, the foundation, then it does us no good at all to improve the externals.

If in building our hearts, our relationship with God, we have fear of the unknown, if when we give our hearts to the Lord we are unsure of what God asks of us, what God's will is for us, let us know that we are not alone. We can take consolation in the words of the great Trappist master of spirituality, Thomas Merton who wrestled with the same fear. "My Lord God," Merton wrote, "I have no idea where I am going. I do not see the road ahead of me. I cannot know for certain where it will end. Nor do I really know myself, and the fact that I think I am following your will does not mean that I am actually doing so. But I believe that the desire to please you does in fact please you. And I hope I have that desire in all that I am doing."[4] May our hearts burn with a similar fire as we journey in our walk of faith in the discovery of God's will today and to eternal life tomorrow.

Question: Am I more concerned with the tangibles of life of do I realize my need for God?

Scripture Passage: "For where you treasure is, there you heart will be also." (Matthew 6:21)

Prayer: Lord, give me a grateful heart so I may love you more fully.

---

[4] Thomas Merton, *Thoughts in Solitude* (New York: The Noonday Press, 1958), 83.

What We Do Matters

An army chaplain encountered a wounded soldier lying in pain in a foxhole. With his Bible in hand, the chaplain came forward and said, "Would you like me to read something from the Bible, the good book?" The soldier could only answer, "I am very thirsty; may I have a drink of water?" The chaplain dutifully went off, found a canteen and poured the soldier a cup of water. The man then began to squirm about as if he was very uncomfortable. Again the chaplain without a second thought took his overcoat, rolled it up, and placed it under the man's head like a pillow. The soldier then began to shiver. "I am so cold," he said. The chaplain wasted no time and shed his own jacket and placed it over the man. Then the soldier said, "Now if there is anything in that book which will allow one to do more for another then you have already done, then please read it because I would like to hear it."

Three students were discussing new translations of the Bible. The first said, "I like the New American Bible. It is clear and easier to read than others." The second suggested, "I like the Jerusalem Bible. It is clear as well, but also poetic and better to use in prayer." The third student said, "I like my mother's version best. She translated the Bible into action so we can better apply it to our lives."

A group of young Christians attended a summer camp where discussions were held on how best to propagate Jesus' Gospel message. In their lively discussion the participants used television, videos, books, essays, and all sorts of printed matter. When they ran out of things to say, one young African women rose and voiced her opinion: "In my country when a pagan village is ready for Christianity we do not send books, money or even a missionary. We send the best Christian family we can find. A good family living the Gospel message is more valuable then all the books in the world."

These three different stories but one central idea. Our actions count; what we do is important. People are either drawn closer to or driven further away from us by what we do and say. People are not neutral in their opinions of others. Witnessing and sharing—they are two simple ideas, but they are the basic tools of evangelization, the process of bringing others closer to God.

Sacred Scripture abounds with passages which describe the ministry of evangelization, but not all incidents are so obvious. The author of the apocalyptic book of Daniel (12:1-3) speaks of those who are enlightened, those who have gained knowledge of God. These are special people; they will shine brightly. The enlightened have a special mission—to bring the many to justice. In this task the enlightened learn something of themselves, of others and of God. God initiates the divine revelation in us, but through our effort we learn something about God as well. Yes, we are called to gather the many; we are called to be evangelists.

The Gospel of Mark provides a second example of gathering those who are special. The angels of God will go to the four corners of the world, to the fours winds to gather those who have been chosen. Who are the chosen? They are us. God has chosen all people for all time, but, unfortunately many do not reciprocate and choose God. As well as being the chosen we have the task of the angels. We are to gather in those chosen by God. Yes, we have the task of being evangelists.

When we hear the word evangelization certain images are brought to mind. First, I think, is the image of the soap-box preacher, with Bible in hand, who gives the congregation Hell-fire and brimstone. We think of the great temperance preachers of the latter part of the nineteenth and early part of the twentieth centuries, the Elmer Gantry of literature and the Father Mathew Theobald and Carrie Nation of history. We also think of the door-to-door sale of religion. Various Christian denominations disagree on certain theological questions, but all admire the great fervor, zeal, and spirit shown by those who have the courage to go door-to-door in the proclamation of Jesus' message.

These are outward, more obvious, and traditional forms of evangelization. But if the essential work of evangelization is to bring others closer to God, and at least initiate the conversion process to Jesus' Gospel message, then all that we do each day is a vehicle of evangelization. We need do nothing out of the ordinary to be an evangelist, but we must be ever mindful and aware that all we do and say is important. If we are in the work place—are the attitudes we bring, the methods that we use in doing our daily tasks ones where the presence of Christ can be seen and recognized? If we are in school—do we treat our teachers and fellow students with respect? Are others attracted to us because we have the courage to stand tall for what we believe or does peer pressure get to us and we compromise both who we are and what we believe to the demons of expediency or acceptance? For all of us, do others see the face of Christ in us, or are our colleagues, friends and family confused because they receive mixed signals in what we say and do?

God's work has been initiated, but it requires completion. Many of us are familiar with the some of the great master works of music, such as Mozart's Requiem or Puccini's great opera Turandot, which were left unfinished due to the death of their creators. But the compositions were completed by the disciples of these great composers. In a similar way Jesus initiated the process of evangelization, the concept of bringing others closer to God 2000 years ago. There were initially twelve, then seventy-two, and then many more. But Jesus is no longer physically present and thus we who bear the name Christian, we who are his disciples, must do our share to complete the task. Therefore, let us witness and share our lives of faith with others. Let us bring others closer to God. Let us gather the harvest and in the process bring the Kingdom of God more fully to our world.

Question: Are people drawn closer to or pushed further from God when they observe me?

Scripture Passage: "If any want to become my followers, let them deny themselves and take up their cross and follow me." (Matthew 16:24)

Prayer: Father, help me to always understand my role in bringing others to Christ, your Son.

Carrying the Tradition

The date was June 22, 1943; the place was the Bronx in New York City. George Herman "Babe" Ruth stood at home plate at fabled Yankee Stadium for the last time. The great Bambino had come to bid farewell to the people of New York and the world of baseball. In addition, Babe Ruth came to instruct and inspire those left behind, those who were to carry on the tradition.

In fifteen seasons with the Yankees Babe Ruth had amassed an impressive record. Before the amazing 1998 season of slugger Mark McGwire, he hit more home runs in a single 154 game season than any player in history; he drew more walks than anyone. Ruth is the only person to hit three home runs in a single world series game. His career record of 714 home runs was only eclipsed in 1974 by another great slugger and Hall of Fame member, Henry Aaron. Babe Ruth was the anchor, the cornerstone to his team. The concept of unity was important to the Yankees. They possessed a certain *esprit de corps*, a certain spirit which they called "the pride of the Yankees." Babe Ruth started a tradition which was manifest in a string of American League pennants and World Series championships. The Babe also left a legacy, in the form of an edifice. Baseball fans call Yankee Stadium, "the house that Ruth built."

Many players inspired by the career and words of Babe Ruth followed in his foot steps; they carried on the tradition. Their names are familiar to most people, especially those who love the game of baseball: Lou Gehrig, Joe Dimaggio, Mickey Mantle, Roger Maris, Whitey Ford, Yogi Berra, Bobby Richardson,

Phil Rizzutto, and the famous manager Casey Stengel. In more recent days the names of Alex Rodriguez, Derrick Jeter, and Roger Clemens have continued the tradition. All of these players have been proud to wear the pinstripe of Yankee blue.

As we all know there have been many famous farewell speeches in history. Although it might sound odd, I am sure that the most famous was spoken by Jesus of Nazareth. Chapters 15 through 17 of St. John's Gospel relate Jesus' farewell address to his disciples and to the world. Jesus says good-bye and instructs his followers on how they are to carry on the tradition in his absence. If the chronology of John's Gospel is correct, then Jesus spent three years in his public ministry with the disciples. During that period his reputation grew. People came from far and near to hear his words and witness his deeds. Jesus gathered quite a following. The record which he amassed during his career, like that of Babe Ruth, was quite amazing. He turned water into wine, raised the dead to new life, including his friend Lazarus, walked on the Sea of Galilee, and calmed a raging storm with only a few words and a simple gesture.

Jesus gathered a team, a community around him during his public ministry. Initially the team consisted of the twelve apostles. But, as was predicted, one of the twelve, Judas, betrayed the cause and was lost. The apostles knew that unity had to be preserved, in order to carry on the tradition. Thus, as we remember from the Acts of the Apostles (1:15-26), the eleven met and chose one who had walked in the footsteps of the Lord during his earthly life. Lots were drawn and Matthias was chosen over Barsabbas to join the eleven.

Jesus and his first followers also left a legacy, the Church. All of us are the Church, the Body of Christ. Jesus, during his life with us protected the Church, so that none would be lost. As he prepared to leave our world, he prayed that God would protect the Church from the evil one, Satan. "O Father, protect them in your name that you have given me, so that they may be one, as we are one." (John 17:11b) We know that God has always existed and believe that he will always be the protector and benefactor of the Church. God's presence and providence sustain us as we live our Christian lives as the Church in our world.

Many men and women, inspired by the life of Jesus and His message, have followed the tradition and been his disciples. Their names are familiar to us all: Augustine, Benedict, Francis and Clare, Dominic, Catherine of Siena, Teresa of Avila, Ignatius of Loyola, and in more recent days Elizabeth Ann Seton, Frances Cabrini, and Maximilian Kolbe. All have been privileged to wear the badge of Jesus' ignominious death, the cross.

Yes, Jesus gave his farewell address to his disciples and to us, but Christ did not leave us orphans; we were never abandoned. No, Jesus left us with all that we need so as to carry his message to the world. We have the unity which the Church provides; we have the tradition. Through evangelization, the process by which we draw others closer to God and at least initiate their conversion, we go forward armed with the truth to do God's work. What exactly is the truth? God's word is the truth. The tradition is also the truth. Truth is found in the magisterium, the teaching office of the Pope and bishops. In other words the truth is God's revelation to God's people. We bring God's word, the tradition, and the magisterium to people most fully through an attitude of love. One might think that love is a rather simple solution to a complex process, but love is all encompassing; love is God. St. John (I John 4:16b) reminds us, "God is love, and those who abide in love abide in God, and God abides in them."

Jesus challenged the disciples to go forward and convert the world. Christ asks us through our baptismal commitment to do the same. We have the tradition; we have the legacy which is the Church. We have the opportunity to be regularly nourished for our task with Christ's Body and Blood. Let us, therefore, go forward, armed with the truth and the certainty of God's presence with us, to bring God's message to all people. Let us do as God has commanded. And let us know that we will be successful for as Jesus said, "You will know the truth, and the truth will make you free." (John 8:32)

Question: Do I seek the truth in my life or do I intentionally hide from it?

Scripture Passage: "That they may all be one. As you, Father, are in me, and I am in you, may they also be in us, so the world may believe that you have sent me." (John 17:21)

Prayer: Jesus, help me to be a team player with you in building your kingdom.

Section II
Daily Human Struggles

Introduction

One of the most memorable programs of Bishop Fulton Sheen's popular 1950s television series, "Life is Worth Living," was titled, "The Psychology of the Rat Race." In his presentation Sheen described how people often avoid the past and have no apparent concern for the future. These people live day-by-day and become completely absorbed in the here and now. Their lives turn inward and the fast pace of contemporary society dominates them. The "Rat Race" has claimed more victims.

The true Christian must live by considering the past and with an ever-present eye to the future. The past provides us with much information on how to live today and tomorrow. If we are wise we learn from our own mistakes and those of others. Experience tells us how to avoid certain pitfalls and detours so we can take the better routes that lead us where we want to be. We must always keep our eyes fixed on the goal which is life eternal. We must always remember St. Paul's powerful forecast (I Corinthians 2:9): "What no eye has seen, nor ear heard, nor the human heart conceived, what God has prepared for those who love him." We are here for one ultimate purpose, to return home to God. Thus, we must never take our eyes off this goal.

While Christians seek not be live of the world, they must live in the world; there is no escape from the reality of our day-to-day lives. Thus, we must not shirk nor try to avoid the struggles that come our way as part of the human condition. On the contrary, we must seek as best we can, to embrace and use them to our advantage. They say there is no such thing as a free lunch. The world can be at times very difficult and thus we must learn how to successfully negotiate the daily struggles that come our way. This is the reality of our world; this is the original sin, the basic human condition into which we are all born. But how we react to these daily struggles and the avenues we take to seek solutions will make all the difference in the world.

The reflections in this section describe some of the day-to-day struggles that are endemic to contemporary life and ways we might better deal with them. It is a daily struggle, especially in our highly secularized world, to stay loyal to God's call and message, especially when we are bombarded with other alternatives and solutions. All of us have many responsibilities in our lives, some of which we might not want for they are like crosses which burden us terribly. Our daily struggle is to see responsibility and privilege as one entity and find ways to grow from what seems an untenable situation or an unfair hardship or responsibility. The cry of the poor daily echoes in our ears, but are we listening so we can assist others. Our lives at home and our place of business provide us with authority and tempt us to use it improperly or even abuse it. We must daily struggle to keep our focus on the goal of Christ and use all of our gifts wisely toward that end. Daily struggles and burdens can be a great trial, but they can also be a source of strength. The attitude we take and the methods we use to negotiate these daily hurdles will determine our way. How will you respond? The choice is in your hands.

Encountering Christ the Merciful One

The Atlantic slave trade was, unquestionably, one of the darkest hours in human history. Between 1450 and 1850 an estimated eighteen million sub-Saharan Africans were ferried from their homeland, with twelve million arriving in the New World. Whether these men and women were sold to traders, kidnaped, or obtained as a booty of war, they were all moved against their will and placed in roles of total servitude. African slaves, from the time of their purchase in Africa to their sale in the Americas, were treated in the most inhumane ways, but it was the voyage to the New World, known by historians as the Middle Passage, that was most gruesome. Slaves were herded aboard vessels and shackled in their places below decks. The average male was given a mere seven square feet of space. The air was foul and made one nauseous, food and water were minimal, and disease was rampant. Often as many as 25% of the Africans died before they ever reached their destinations. When they arrived their condition was, as one can only imagine, poor. The wretched conditions and inhuman treatment were characteristic of the mentality concerning slaves; they were property, not human beings.

Cartegena, located along the northern coast of what is today Colombia, was a major port of debarkation for slave vessels. While the Church was established in the region by the late sixteenth century, few ecclesiastical officials ever questioned slavery let alone reached out to those who, through no wish of their own, were forced to participate. In 1610, however, a

Spanish Jesuit named Peter Claver, arrived in Cartegena and quickly took up a personal ministry to the approximately 10,000 Black Africans who arrived annually. When a slave ship arrived the men, women, and children onboard were herded on shore and placed in pens like animals, without any medical attention or other assistance. Peter Claver, imitating the work of his mentor, Fr. Alfonso de Sandoval, took the time necessary to visit the slaves and attended to their physical needs with food and medicine. When the slaves were sent to the mines, as was generally the case on the west coast of South America, Claver went along to assist them, generally without the permission of owners, placing himself in jeopardy. He was not concerned about what others thought of him, all that mattered was that his service was needed. Peter Claver called himself, "the slave of the slaves for ever." Many had the opportunity to help but seemed to ignore the situation. Others may have noticed but did not have the courage to act.

Peter Claver's ministry to African slaves did not preclude him from caring for others, including condemned criminals whom he prepared for death, visiting local hospitals, and conducting an annual mission to traders and seamen in the region. Through his efforts many Africans slaves and others found the faith.

When Peter Claver died in 1654 he was recognized with a huge funeral arranged by the slaves and others he assisted. He was canonized in 1888 and declared at the time the patron of all missionary enterprises among Black Africans. He was a man who when given the opportunity to encounter one less fortunate than himself did precisely what Jesus commands in the Scriptures, he treated them with mercy. We are challenged to do the same.

The famous parable of the Good Samaritan (Luke 10:25-37) presents a situation that forces us to ask: If we were given a special chance to be a neighbor and show mercy, how would we respond? In the story a man traveling from Jerusalem to Jericho, a treacherous and dangerous route even today, falls among thieves who rob and beat him severely. The man is so badly injured he is unable to care for himself. The parable, which might be appropriately titled, "The man who took the opportunity to encounter God by showing mercy," presents three men who are given the chance to help and befriend the injured man, thereby encountering God by showing mercy. The first two, the priest and the Levite, were highly respected members of the community, the kind of people society appreciates and in whom trust is placed. These two, one-by-one, come upon the scene. They have the opportunity to help, but they do not take advantage of the opportunity afforded them. As St. Luke says, they simply passed by. The third man who comes upon the scene is a Samaritan, a descendent of one of the "ten lost tribes" of the Northern Kingdom of Israel, conquered by the Assyrians 700 years before Christ. Jews did not trust Samaritans; they were not accepted in Hebrew society nor considered worthy of respect. Yet, this third man, the one who everyone hated and was given no respect or chance in life, was the one who took the opportunity God gave to him, to be neighbor and to show mercy to another.

The New Testament is filled with numerous accounts of how Jesus demonstrated mercy toward others. The Lord said that his mission was to the lost sheep of Israel, yet when pressed by the Syro-Phoencician who demonstrated great faith (Mark 7:24-30) Jesus displayed mercy and cured the woman's daughter. On two occasions Jesus fed the crowds (the five thousand—Mark 6:3-44, Matthew 14:13-21, Luke 9:10-17, John 6:1-15 and the four thousand—Matthew 15:32-39 and Mark 8:1-10) who had come to hear his message. He had compassion on the people for he saw them as sheep without a shepherd. We recall as well how Jesus reached out to the woman caught in the act of adultery (John 8:1-11). Instead of standing in accusation as did the religious leaders of the time, Jesus challenged them so severely that not one was able to cast a stone, knowing that none was without sin. Jesus never claimed the woman was innocent; this was not the point of his intervention. Rather, his action taught that people must be compassionate. Christ lived his life totally for others and his ministry was centered in compassion. John (8:11) reports the Lord's conversation with the adulterous woman: "'Woman, where are they? Has no one condemned you?' She said, 'No one, sir.' And Jesus said, 'Neither do I condemn you. Go your way, and from now on do not sin again.'"

God gives us many chances and opportunities to demonstrate a God-like compassion toward others. Have we taken advantage of the possibilities God has sent our way, or do we merely pass by? The opportunity to be a neighbor, to show that we care and in the process show the face of God to others happens each day. Almost daily we encounter people who are hurt. It may be a person who hurts physically, like the man who fell among robbers, but more often we will find people who hurt inside, someone who has been wounded by the words and actions of others, by events, or the cruelty of the world.

When someone hurts or wants to talk, do we do as the priest and Levite and pass by or do we take the time and make the effort of the Samaritan and show God to others. When we have acted inappropriately in the eyes of God and/or society do we stand in accusation of others like those who attacked the adulterous woman or, are we mindful of Jesus' admonition to take the plank from our own eye before we remove the splinter from our neighbor's? (Matthew 7:3-5) Should we not be more like Jesus who came to bind up and heal and not to tear down? We cannot be there always for others—there would be nothing left for ourselves. But what is our attitude? Is our heart open like the Samaritan or closed like the priest and Levite? Each person must answer!

Compassion requires us to foster a spirit of reconciliation in our lives. In the Letter to the Colossians (1:20), the Pauline author says we are all reconciled in Christ, but are we reconciled with one another? Does everyone have an equal chance with us, or have some been written off as society wrote off the unfortunate African slave? Have we written off individuals or groups as lazy, unproductive, or not useable? Have we said in essence, I don't need you; I will just pass you by? This tendency can happen with all of us whatever our age may be. Children by ignoring their friends or refusing friendship say I don't need you; you are not my neighbor. Adults who continually refuse to respond to God's call found in the faces and voices of neighbors, the sick, the poor, the stranger say, I don't need you; you are not my neighbor. When we always care more for ourselves and seemingly forget the needs of others, we say is essence, you are not important; I will pass you by. In such cases what opportunities we miss. God is so near; we only need to open our eyes and see him!

Answering the call of the Lord to be neighbor is not too difficult when we know and like an individual or believe that our actions will one day result in some reciprocity. When, on the other hand, we sense that nothing will come our way in return we at times hesitate. We must remember Jesus' admonition not to seek reward: "So you also, when you have done all that you have been ordered to do, say, 'We are worthless slaves; we have done only what we ought to have done.'" (Luke 17: 10)

Peter Claver ran afoul of civic and religious leaders and endured conditions that others would not even consider in carrying out Jesus' edict to be neighbor and not pass by. He knew he would get nothing in return, but that did not change his response. Are we ready for the challenge? Can we stop long enough to be a true neighbor to a person in need, physically, emotionally or spiritually? Can we respond to the Lord's exhortation on mercy, "Go and do likewise?" Only you can answer.

Question: When was the last time I took the opportunity to befriend someone in need, especially a stranger?

Scripture Passage: "For the Lord is compassionate and merciful; he forgives sins and saves in time of distress." (Sirach 2:11)

Prayer: Lord, help me to be compassionate to all, but especially those most in need of your care.

What Are You Willing to Do For Me?

In the fifteenth century a rural village in Germany was home to a family with 18 children. The family was poor, but despite the difficulty of making ends meet, two brothers in the family still held a dream, namely to pursue their talent as artists. With the financial situation bleak the two boys came up with their own solution to the problem. They agreed to toss a coin with the loser going to the local mines to work so he could support the other while he attended art school. When the first was finished with his training, he would support the education of the other, either by sale of his art works or by going to the mines himself. Thus, one brother went off to the dangerous mines while the other went to the art academy. After four years the young artist returned triumphantly to a homecoming dinner. The artist rose from the table to drink a toast to his beloved brother for his years of sacrifice. He said, "Now Albert, it is your turn to go to the Academy and pursue your dream; I will support you."

Albert sat at the table and tears began to flow down his cheeks. He could only say, "No, no, no." Finally Albert rose, wiped the tears from his face, and holding his hands out in front of him said softly, "No, brother, it is too late for me to go. Look at my time in the mines has done to my hands. The bones in every finger have been crushed at least once and I suffer from arthritis so severely that I cannot even hold a wine glass properly to return your toast, much less make lines on a canvas with pen or brush. No, brother, for me it is too late."

Then, one day to pay homage to his brother who had sacrificed his dream for him, the great artist Albrecht Durer painstakingly drew his brothers hands with palms together and crooked fingers pointed skyward. He called his powerful painting simply "Hands" but the entire world almost immediately opened its heart to the masterpiece and renamed his great work and tribute of love "The Praying Hands."

The true story of the creation of one of Albrecht Durer's master paintings depicts how far one man was willing to go for another. Albert Durer's sacrifice for his brother gave the world a treasured masterpiece. Scripture calls us to consider how far are we willing to go for another; how much can we sacrifice to assist others and promote the work of Christ in our world?

The Gospels provide many examples of great sacrifice. In the story of the widow's mite (Luke 21:1-4) we hear how Jesus commends this woman's great sacrifice. While many rich people contributed sizeable amounts of money to the Temple treasury she gave only two copper coins. But her gift was much greater; she gave what she did not have to give. She did not give from her surplus like the others; on the contrary she gave from her want. She went beyond what anyone would expect. The Syro-Phoenician woman (Mark 7:24-30) presents another example of sacrifice. Although not a Jew, she had the courage to come to Jesus and ask him to assist her daughter. She was willing to undergo ridicule from her own people as well as the challenge of Jesus himself to obtain relief for her daughter. Jesus rewards her faith; her sacrifice brings healing for her child. Undoubtedly the best example of sacrifice is the life of Mary of Nazareth. From her great fiat, "Here I am, the servant of the Lord; let it be with me, according to your word" (Luke 1:38a) to her vigil beneath the cross (John 19:25-27), she was a woman of sorrow who sacrificed her life for her Son and family. She had no idea what her role in God's plan of salvation would require, but she was willing to sacrifice so that God's will could be accomplished.

Assuredly the great people of faith described in the Gospels were rewarded because of their sacrifice. They are surely part of the elect described in the Book of Revelation (14:1-5). These women of faith, and many more, have ransomed the world because they were found without deceit or flaw. Their sacrifices brought them to the eternal life which is the gift for all who believe.

Few if any of us will be called to go to the mines to support our siblings, other family members or friends. None of us, most probably, will have to give from our want or need to support the Church on any other institution that seeks our assistance. But the question must be asked—how far are we willing to go? What are we prepared to do? How much will we inconvenience ourselves for the needs of others? These are challenging questions because they force us to move off our beds of complacency and area of comfortableness and see how much we trust in God to provide what we don't have. Are we willing to take the time we don't have to meet the need of the family member, associate at work, or neighbor down the street? Possibly more important are we willing to assist the fellow traveler on the road whom we do not know, but whose need is great—the alien, the sick and diseased, aged, and homeless—in short those whom society has placed on the fringe and declared unapproachable? Can we go beyond ourselves for others?

We are very comfortable assisting God's people on our own terms, schedule, and time frame. We cannot do everything and meet all needs. We cannot and do not have to save the world; Jesus did that once for all time. But do we have the courage, strength and faith to go beyond giving from our excess time, talent, treasure, and opportunity, and truly answer God's call to serve and sacrifice? Are we willing, as demonstrated so powerfully in the famous apocalyptic passage from Matthew chapter 25, to be servants to the least of our brothers and sisters, even if not convenient or uncomfortable?

To be the best servants and to go the extra mile for another, as did Albert Durer for his brother, will generate some pain, but only through the pain can we understand the sacrifice to which we are all called. The legend of the Emille Bell demonstrates what we must do:

There was an ancient temple bell famous for its beautiful tone. It had been commissioned by a king as a way of showing his devotion to Buddha. The king's advisors had told him that making a huge bell in honor of the Buddha would secure the nation from foreign invasion. So the king approached the most competent and talented bell maker in the realm with his request. The man worked hard and produced many bells, but none was extraordinary; none had the special tone that was necessary.

Finally the bell maker went to the king and told him that the only way to get the kind of bell he wanted was to sacrifice a young maiden. Soldiers were sent to find and fetch a young girl. Coming upon a poor mother in a farm village with her young daughter, they took the child away, while the girl cried aloud, "Emille! Emille!—Mother, O mother!" When the molten lead and iron were prepared, the girl was thrown in. At last the bell maker had succeeded.

The bell, called the Emille Bell, made a sound more beautiful than any other. When it rang most people praised the artist who had produced such a sound, but whenever the woman whose child had been sacrificed heard it, her heart broke anew. Her neighbors, who knew her great sacrifice and pain, could not hear the beautiful tone without the pain, either. Only those who understand the sacrifice can feel the pain. Others simply enjoy the sound. Let us not simply hear the sound, let us feel the pain of others as we journey the path toward Christ and eternal life.

Question: Am I willing to inconvenience myself in order to assist another?

Scripture Passage: "Rejoice in hope, be patient in suffering, persevere in prayer." (Romans 12:12)

Prayer: Lord, never allow me to be selfish, but to always be willing to sacrifice my needs or wants for those of others.

Preparing the Way of the Lord

One day a mighty and majestic pine tree, the tallest tree in the whole forest, said to a little squirrel playing in its branches, "There is a great treasure waiting for you at my top most branch, if you are willing to make the journey in order to find it." Now this great pine tree was itself a great treasure. It produced some of the meatiest and tastiest pine nuts in the forest and it provided shelter for many animals that called the forest home. This little squirrel was inquisitive, however, and she wondered what the great treasure might be. She decided at that moment that she would take the journey so as to discover the great treasure.

The trip would be long and because the squirrel was wise and possessed forethought she knew planning was required. Food had to be taken on the journey. Thus, she chose from her nest some of the best and most delicious nuts that she had stored. She placed them in a little satchel and tied it around her waist. Then she began to climb. At the base of the tree the branches were full and the pine nuts were plentiful, but as she rose higher and higher in the tree, the branches became thinner and thinner and the pine nuts fewer and fewer. She stopped for a moment and rested. She was happy that she had brought food along on the trip. She took out a nut and enjoyed a little snack. This trip was more difficult then she had anticipated. She thought about returning home, but the commitment had been made and she would complete the journey.

As she climbed higher and higher she wondered what the great treasure might be? Maybe she should have asked the tree. But when she looked up she thought she saw the top. There was no need to ask now; soon she would find out for herself. After another half hour of climbing she made it to the top and clung to the top most branch as it swayed in the wind. She looked around for the treasure, but could see nothing. She thought there might be a giant pine nut or at least one which was delightful to the eye; she saw nothing like this. Had the tree tricked her? Disappointed, frustrated, and now tired and hungry, she prepared to return home. Thus, she turned around, hung upside down, as squirrels often do, and made ready to climb down. But when she looked down the view that she beheld was truly amazing. She could see for miles, every valley and mountain, every stream and river. Because this was the tallest tree she could see without any obstruction. This was better than any pine nut could possibly be.

She wanted to stay there forever, but realized because the climb had been long and difficult that the sun would set in a few hours and she needed to return home by nightfall. Thus, renewed in spirit, if not in body, she made the easier trip down the tree. That night when speaking to all the other squirrels she told them about her adventure, and it is said by all her friends that she was never hungry again.[5]

Like the squirrel who undertook a difficult journey in order to find a great treasure, so all the Christian community moves day-by-day along the path which leads to the discovery of the

---

[5] Paraphrased from "The Squirrel and the Pine Tree," in John Aurelio, *Colors! Stories of the Kingdom* (New York: Crossroad, 1993), 63-64.

greatest treasure of all—Jesus Christ. We should know that peoples long before our time took similar journeys in order to find God. Scripture tells us about these journeys.

Baruch was a prophet who spoke to the Hebrew people in exile in Babylon. The people had been away from their homeland for a long time; many probably thought that God had abandoned them. Baruch tells the people that if they want to find God and return home they must build a highway. It is not a highway made of cement, asphalt, and stone, like the roads of today. No, this is a highway in their minds. The prophet writes, "Arise , O Jerusalem, stand upon the height; look toward the east, and see your children gathered from west to east at the word of the Holy One, rejoicing that God has remembered them....For God has ordered that every high mountain and the everlasting hills be made low and the valleys filled up, to make level ground, so that Israel may walk safely in the glory of God....For God will lead Israel with joy, in the light of his glory, with the mercy and righteousness that come from God." (Baruch 5: 5,7,9) The reason the people could not find God was that their minds were too full of other things; God was not that important. Baruch tells the people to remove those things that are unimportant and make a path to God that is level, smooth, and straight. Then the people will find God and they will return home.

John the Baptist was another prophet who delivered a similar message to a different group of people. John spoke to the Hebrews of his day and told them that they too must build a highway in order to find God: "Prepare the way of the Lord; make his paths straight. Every valley shall be filled, and every mountain and hill shall be made low; and the crooked shall be made straight, and the rough ways made smooth." (Luke 3:4b-5) Jesus, the one for whom John was to prepare the way, was present, but the people would not find him unless they prepared themselves.

We have all learned in high school geometry that the shortest distance between any two points is a straight line. Life is full of journeys which require us to move between points A and B. Some of the journeys are physical and it may be possible to move in a direct path, a straight line. But the most important journeys in life, such as our journey through school, the road of moving from the single life to marriage and family, or our movement from being a working person to retirement, are seldom if ever negotiated in a straight line. No, we rise to the heights of success and triumph and we at times enter the valley of defeat and despair. We come to a fork in the road and we choose the right path only to find that it is really a detour and more difficult and time consuming than if we had chosen to go to the left.

We must do the best we can to make level, smooth, and straight our highway that leads to God. The little squirrel realized that her long journey would require some planning and thus she brought food along with her. So the Church provides opportunities to prepare ourselves as we journey toward God. We have the liturgical seasons, the sacraments, Scripture, and the Christian community itself. These give insight, guidance and strength on our journey toward salvation and eternal life with God.

All of us, like the squirrel are on the tree and we are climbing toward our goal. God willing we will make it to the top. But when we get there, turn upside down and look out what will we see? Hopefully we can see the enormity of God's love manifest in so many ways, all of which help to guide us home. Let us continue on the road blazed by Christ and the countless saints who have followed his path. Let us walk the road to Jesus and eternal life.

Question: Do I possess sufficient faith to walk the more difficult road, or do I take the easy detour?

Scripture Passage: "Enter through the narrow gate; for the gate is wide and the road is easy that leads to destruction, and there are many who take it. For the gate is narrow and the road is hard that leads to life, and there are few who find it." (Matthew 7:13-14)

Prayer: Lord, help me to walk the road less traveled, but the only path that leads to You.

Allowing God to Change Us

"Hoke, you are my best friend." It took Daisy Werthan almost twenty years to make that statement; it wasn't easy. The relationship between Daisy and Hoke was not mutual or cordial at the outset. Daisy had driven her beautiful 1948 Packard into her neighbor's backyard. Boolie Werthan, Daisy's son, thought that such an incident was sufficient evidence to warrant that his mother stop driving; she needed a driver, a chauffeur. Hoke Coleburn, a middle-aged Black man, was Boolie's choice for the job. Daisy, however, would not accept this restriction, this change in her life; she was not open to being transformed.

Boolie may have hired Hoke but that did not mean that Miss Daisy had to use his service. As Hoke stood idly by, Miss Daisy took the street car wherever she went, to the hair dresser, to the grocery store. Hoke Coleburn was being paid for doing nothing. That is exactly how Miss Daisy wanted things.

As stubborn as she could be, Miss Daisy ultimately did change her attitude. One day she needed a few things from the store. She left the house and began to walk toward the street car. Hoke decided that Miss Daisy's refusal to use his services needed to end. As she walked down the sidewalk Hoke slowly drove alongside in the new 1948 Hudson Boolie had purchased for his mother. "Where are you going," scowled Daisy. Hoke replied, "I'm fixin' to take you to the store!" Although still not contend with the arrangement, Daisy agreed to get into the car; her conversion had begun.

Daisy did not approve, but Hoke had become her chauffeur. Whether it was to the Temple, you see Miss Daisy was Jewish, the store, or a trip to Mobile, Alabama to visit relatives, Daisy and Hoke went together. As the years passed their relationship as driver and passenger grew; they became bonded together. Then one day Miss Daisy's long and sometimes difficult conversion became complete with her statement of faith, "Hoke, you are my best friend."

Alfred Uhry's 1988 Pulitzer Prize winning play and popular movie "Driving Miss Daisy" is more than a story of a chauffeur and an elderly rich widow. It is a story of the process of transformation and acceptance in one's life. Scripture challenges us to transform our lives in order to gain greater personal knowledge and understanding of God.

The book of Genesis (12:1-4) describes how Abram was asked by God to go forth, to venture out, to find change, and be converted. What God asked of Abram could not have been easy. He was an old man, yet he was asked to leave his home, his livelihood, everything that he knew. God had given him a promise, a special blessing, that he would be the father of a great nation one day. Even with such a promise, however, Abram would not have been able to act if he had not been a man of faith. Abram was able to believe that God was calling him to change for some good reason.

The Synoptic accounts of Jesus' transfiguration (Matthew 17:1-8, Luke 9:28-36, and Mark 9:2-8) illustrate our need for transformation. Theologians debate about this passage in Scripture. Some say it was an actual event; many think it was a special spiritual experience of the apostles. Some theologians think the story is a misplaced post-resurrection account of how the apostles experienced Jesus. All three synoptic Gospel evangelists, Matthew, Mark, and Luke, tell us about this event in

Jesus' life. This fact alone makes this passage highly significant. What is the importance? We are told that Jesus was transfigured; his clothes became dazzlingly white; his physical appearance was radiant. In a few minutes the event ended; Jesus' physical appearance returned to normal. The change, the transformation which occurred with the three favored apostles, Peter, James and John, is, however, what is most significant. Their experience of seeing Jesus changed their lives forever.

The Christian life is a constant challenge to welcome the opportunities for transformation that enter our lives. We can look at three traditional disciplines of our Faith and see how they can help us along the path which leads to transformation in our lives. Almsgiving is the first discipline. We need to believe that works of mercy are necessary. How can we change our schedules or daily lives so as to make almsgiving something that is possible in what we do? Do we need to change our attitudes about almsgiving which may hold us back from full participation?

Fasting is a second discipline. Do we need to change our eating habits permanently? Do we need to eliminate certain items from our life, things which ultimately cause us harm—drugs, drink, tobacco? Can we transform our lives to be in solidarity with those who are less fortunate than most of us when it comes to material possessions?

Prayer is a third traditional Christian discipline. Can we change our priorities if needed so as to assure we make time for conversation with our God, today and each day? Are we willing to try new methods of prayer in order to make our conversation with the Lord more fruitful and fulfilling? Can we let the word of God become part of us, to enter deep down so as to later blossom forth as God's love directed toward others?

Each day we have the opportunity to encounter the Lord. As we journey along the Christian road, let us allow the encounters we have with God change us; let each encounter be the opportunity for transformation. Let us accept the change that God asks of us, like Abram, like Miss Daisy in Alfred Uhry's play. Let our encounter with God change us forever!

Question: What aspect of my life needs to be transformed the most?

Scripture Passage: "Rend your hearts and not your clothing. Return to the Lord, your God." (Joel 2:13)

Prayer: Father, help me to be open to the conversion which only you can bring.

Loyalty to God or the World?

He was a man of mystery and charm; he was a man of brokenness and faith. He was hunted down, like a common criminal. His only crime it seems was seeking God's glory. The "Whiskey Priest" lived in Southern Mexico. The time was the 1920s; the Cristero Rebellion was underway. The Whiskey Priest was not perfect—far from it. He drank too much; he fathered a child. In those days the government said that is was illegal to practice the priesthood. That, however, did not stop the Whiskey Priest. Everything that he did—the Masses, baptisms, funerals—was conducted in secret.

The Federales and their lieutenant commander represented the government. This band of soldiers possessed the power. It was their job to find the Whiskey Priest, to stop his activity, and ultimately to eliminate him. The hunt went from town to town, village to village. In one village the lieutenant knew the Whiskey Priest had been present, yet the residents would say nothing. The lieutenant was more persuasive; he shot five villagers to loosen their tongues.

The Whiskey Priest was living on borrowed time, but he continued to move from town to town. The winter rains helped him "disappear" in the mountain highlands. The Federales would win, however, it was just a matter of time. In the end he was found, tried and convicted, then executed, a common criminal to the government, but a martyr to the people.

Graham Greene's epic story, *The Power and the Glory* contrasts imperfect humanity struggling for the glory of

God against a society seeking power and the destructive elements derived from it. The ofttimes anti-God orientation of contemporary society presents us with this same challenging option.

In the book of Genesis we hear about how the desire for power was born into the human race. Adam and Eve had all that they needed; they were totally provided for in their existence. Still, they wanted more. They wanted all knowledge; they wanted to become like God. Their desire for power cost them everything. With the knowledge they gained, they lost their innocence. Their desire to be like God only produced problems. Adam and Eve gave into outside pressure. Temptation won; power was triumphant; sin entered the world.

Matthew's Gospel (4:1-11) tells the famous story of Jesus' temptation in the desert. Jesus serves as the contrast to Adam. He is offered the three treasures of our world, but he never gives in to the temptation. The first temptation is power in the offer of changing stones into bread. Power is not necessary for Jesus; concentrating on God's word is more important. Prestige is the second great temptation seen in the challenge to throw himself from the temple. Satan chides Jesus saying that he is an important person and, thus, his angels will care for him. Jesus responds by saying that he does not need to show his prestige. Jesus' prestige is clear; he is God and God shall not be tempted. The final temptation is to wealth in the offer to grant all the kingdoms of the world to Jesus. Just bow down and worship me is the challenge of Satan. Jesus responds that he does not need such riches. Jesus will not honor Satan; God alone is to be worshiped.

St. Paul in writing to the Christian community at Rome (5:12-19) summarizes these important ideas. The Apostle says that through one man, Adam, sin entered the world. It is the original sin, a condition that levels all people. It is the reality that we live in a world which can be filled with joy, but is also many times plagued with problems and pain. But through Jesus the sin of the world is remitted; we are all acquitted. Through the presence of Jesus we can live in this sometimes cruel world and flourish.

As we make our journey through life we must ask ourselves the question, where do we stand, with God or the world? Concerning power—does the desire for control of others consume us? If we have power do we use it for personal gain or for the betterment of all? Is power a thing of value and a necessity, or can we live without it? With regard to prestige—do we do things so others will notice? Do we use our position to dominate others? Or, do we seek the glory of God and not concern ourselves with what society might think? With respect to wealth, are we seeking to out do our neighbor in what we have? Is money the item around which our world revolves? Is money the solution to all our problems? In short, have power, prestige, and money become the gods to which we pay homage?

We need to evaluate our approach to life. Are we the imperfect human, the Whiskey Priest of society, who moves toward the Lord and seeks God's glory? Or, are we the Federales who seek the power of our world? God challenges us today to seek the higher realms; our response is awaited.

Question: What receives my greatest loyalty—God or God's creation?

Scripture Passage: "In the world you face persecution. But take courage; I have overcome the world!" (John 16:33)

Prayer: Loving God, help me to center my life on you and your message of love.

Dying to New Life

If you look up the word paradox in the dictionary you will find a definition that runs something like this: a statement which on first examination appears to be false, but on a closer reading is found to be true. There are many examples of paradoxes, but two can illustrate the concept, one from literature and one from the world of mathematics.

In the famous dialogue "Meno" by Plato, Socrates, the protagonist, and his friend Meno are in a deep discussion. Meno poses the following question, "Is it possible to know that which one has not learned?" Meno answers his own question saying, no. There is nothing that a human knows that has not been previously learned. Socrates, however, looks at this question, known as Meno's Paradox, and says, yes. There are certain things that are so innate to the human person that they are known without learning—things such as breathing, the desire for life, and the emotions of love.

The second paradox is from the world of mathematics. If you want to go from point A to point B and you move exactly one-half of the remaining distance between the two points on each move, you will never arrive at your destination. At first glance you might say, that certainly cannot be correct; I must be able to figure this out. The statement is a paradox. If one can move only half the remaining distance each time, you will come close, infinitesimally close, but you will never arrive.

Although we can all probably think of many other paradoxes, one might ask, what is the greatest of all paradoxes? The answer most assuredly is Christianity. Christ himself is a paradox. Jesus is God, yet he is human at the same time. How is this possible? It is a mystery, yet it is the truth. It is a paradox. Most especially the teaching of Jesus, his message which forms the basis of our faith is a paradox. In John's Gospel Jesus gives us the classic Christian paradox, "Unless a grain of wheat falls to the earth and dies, it remains just a grain of wheat; but if it dies, then it bears much fruit." (John 12:24) Again Jesus says the same thing in different words, "Those who love their life lose it, and those who hate their life in this world will keep it for eternal life." (John 12:25)

How is this possible? It cannot be true we say, but it is. It is a paradox. Yes, the reality is that Jesus' statement is true. More importantly we must ask, what does it mean for us? Do we need to die to find eternal life? Is our life here without merit? Are our efforts this day useless? The meaning and significance of Jesus' statement, this ultimate paradox, is that we are to give our lives for others. This is done through sacrifice. We are to give to others. We are to take less so that others may have some. It is done by sharing what we have in material things. In short, as the expression goes, it is to live simply so others may simply live.

How do we do this; how do we live for others? The principal way that Jesus' life suggests is through service. We are to serve those who are meek and lowly, those who seem to count for little in our world. It is ministry, namely service to the poor and homeless. Our ultimate goal should be to die in Christ and rise to a new, fuller, and eternal life. But this does not mean that we are not accountable now. The Christian paradox is not only for our time of death, it must be lived each day in our relationship with God and God's people.

Jesus' announcement that "the hour has come" challenges us to see that our hour is here as well. It is our hour for action; it is our hour to renew our relationship with God. Dying to the world produces nothing, but to die to self in this world produces many wonderful gifts, such as renunciation, sacrifice, and service. In short, dying to self produces the gifts which lead us to a fuller relationship with God and God's people.

Yes, it is true, Christianity is a paradox. Our life finds its greatest merit through death. Physical death will bring us to the presence of God and eternal life when God calls us to himself. But more importantly death to self now produces much fruit for God's people, and the Kingdom of God is made more manifest each day. Therefore, let be willing to sacrifice; let us be of service to others. Let us die to self, as the Christian paradox calls us to do, and in the process find eternal life as well!

Question: Is generosity a value I demonstrate or is selfishness more the daily reality?

Scripture Passage: "Be generous when you worship the Lord, and do not stint the first fruits of your hands." (Sirach 35:10)

Prayer: Lord, help me to emulate your Son's life by assisting others with their burdens.

Using Authority Properly

Carpe Diem—seize the day. That was the motto John Keating used with his students. He wanted them to make the most of the ability they were given on any particular day. He pushed his students to positive ends with the authority he had been given as a teacher. John had come to Wesley Prep to teach English, especially poetry. His methods were a bit unusual; he gave his students a new approach to learning. He threw out the old methods in a symbolic fashion by ripping pages from old textbooks which in John's mind no longer communicated a positive approach to learning. John Keating gathered his students; they came to listen to him. He brought unity and fun to a discipline where it had been missing for a long time.

Many years ago John Keating himself had been a student at Wesley. During his tenure as a student John and his friends had formed a club to read and enjoy poetry; they called it the Dead Poets Society. Now, twenty years later, John's students gave new life to the Society as they too gathered each night to listen to Longfellow, Tennyson, and other great poets of the past.

John Keating's method was not without conflict. One of Mr. Keating's students had a serious home conflict which began to involve the teacher. The young man wanted to enter upon a career in drama and the theater, but his father wanted him to pursue engineering or business. John Keating supported his student in the youth's desire to be what he wanted. But the young man's father was adamant; his son would never enter into such folly as the theater. The father abused his authority as a parent. He alienated his son and brought discord to the family. In the end the conflict between father and son grew so grave that the young man took his own life. John Keating, with his new methods, his positive approach in support of this young man and his other students, was blamed for the student's death. The administration of Wesley Prep abused its authority and power. The Dead Poets Society was scattered and John Keating was dismissed as a teacher.

The movie Dead Poets Society, produced several years back, tells a story of authority. The film contrasts the use and abuse of power, the gathering and scattering of people. In the writings of the prophet Jeremiah, we hear how the Kings of Israel abused their power. They misused their authority given them by God. The Kings of Israel scattered the flock, that is God's people; they set up barriers which prevented the people from finding God. Jeremiah says that the sheep, the people, were scattered, but God will save the day. "Then I myself will gather the remnant of my flock out of the lands where I have driven them, and I will bring them back to their fold and they shall be fruitful and multiply. I will raise up shepherds over them who will shepherd them, and they shall not fear any longer, or be dismayed, nor shall any be missing, says the Lord." (23:3-4) God will give the people a new leader, from the line of David. His name will be the "The Lord is our righteousness."

Mark's Gospel (6:30-34) tells us about this new leader. It is no surprise to us that Jesus is the one who was sent to re-gather the flock. Jesus is the promise of Jeremiah; he is the promise of all the prophets for all time. People came from all over to see Jesus. Jesus takes pity on them, for as St. Mark describes them, they were sheep without a shepherd. Jesus would be that new shepherd, the one with a positive direction, the one who would gather the sheep in their walk toward God. Jesus started his work with the apostles, but now his ministry extends to all. St. Paul in his Letter to the Ephesians (2:13-18) describes the ministry Jesus performed. The Lord, Paul says, came to break down the barriers which the Kings of Israel had established. Jesus brought together the near, that is the Jews, and the distant, that is the Gentiles, into one common union, one family of God's children. Paul writes, "For this is our peace: in his flesh he has made both groups into one and has broken down the dividing wall, that is, the hostility between us. He has abolished the law with its commandments and ordinances, that he might create in himself one new humanity in place of the two, thus making peace, and might reconcile both groups to God in one body through the cross, thus putting to death that hostility through it." (2:14-16) Jesus used his authority to unify, to make things better, in contrast to the abuse of the Kings of Israel. Jesus came to love all people, not to use them.

Each of us in big or little ways has some authority and we are asked to use it properly. Our authority may be that of a parent exercised over children. The authority we possess may be in the work place, as a supervisor, foreman, manager or group leader. Possibly our authority is found in the community as an elected official, club officer, or volunteer. Maybe the authority we wield is being an older child in a family with multiple siblings. The authority we possess may be a combination of the above.

Each role of authority can be used or abused; the decision is ours. If you are parents—do you unify your family by what you say or do? Does your family benefit from your leadership, from the way you use your authority? Or, do you alienate your children or your spouse? Do you push them away and make them seek solace in others? If you are a supervisor, foreman or manager at work—do your employees benefit from the decisions you make? Is the work place a safe and congenial place for all? Or, do your decisions cause others to leave, to scatter? Do you make the work place intolerable by insensitivity or abuse of authority? If you are a community leader—do your decisions benefit others? Are others better off because you have helped them? Or, do you do your civic duty for the personal benefits which may be reaped from your position? If you are an older brother or sister in the family—do you treat others in the family with respect? Do you love and care for them? Or, do you try to dominate, to lord it over others, to control them, because you are older, wiser and bigger?

The film Dead Poets Society contrasted the use and abuse of authority. John Keating gathered his students into a community. He used his authority and power to get his young students excited about poetry and learning, to help them grow and mature in a positive direction. John Keating used his authority as a teacher wisely. Parents and the school administration, however, abused their positions and hurt others, taking one life and destroying others. Life puts us in positions of authority. Let us be mindful, therefore, to use responsibly the authority and consequent power we have been given. Let us today remember that Jesus came to be a shepherd, to guide, to direct. Jesus came to show us how to use our authority to gather people and move them in a positive, God-centered direction. Jesus came to break down the barriers that keep us from God and to show us love. Let us do the same!

Question: Do I "lord it over" people I know or do I exercise my authority for the betterment of all?

Scripture Passage: "Do not work for the food that perishes, but for the food that endures for life eternal." (John 6:27)

Prayer: Lord, help me to use wisely and properly the authority you have given me.

Making Room for Christ

Hermann Hesse in his wonderful novel *Siddhartha* speaks of the search for life and meaning. It is a story of seeing and ultimately believing. Siddhartha is the son of a Brahmin or religious holy man in the East. One day he goes to his father and asks permission to leave the village of his birth in search of the meaning of life. Initially his father is hesitant to let him go, but the boy presses him and, ultimately, the older man allows his son to leave. Siddhartha and his best friend gather a few belongings and leave the village the next day in search of the meaning of life.

The boys travel less than a day's walk from the village when they come upon a vast and wide river. Siddhartha looks upon the water and realizes the emptiness which lays before him. Certainly, he thinks, this river has no meaning; it is so vast yet so empty. The meaning of life cannot be found here. The two boys hire a ferryman to take them to the other shore and they continue their search.

After a few days of travel the boys come upon a group of ascetics, people who spend much time in prayer and reflection. Siddhartha thinks that the meaning of life might be found here. The boys ask permission from the community leader to join and learn the ways of prayer and meditation. They stay for several years growing from youths to young adults. But after learning the ways of prayer and filling himself with methods of reflection Siddhartha realizes that the meaning of life will not to be found here either. Thus, the two friends move on again.

After a few more day's journey they come upon a Guru or holy man. They are allowed to become the guru's disciples. After a short time, however, Siddhartha knows that the meaning of life for him will not to be found here. His friend, however, finds fulfillment, and thus, the two best friends part company forever.

Siddhartha moves on in his quest to find the meaning of life. He enters a great city, finds work and love as well. He lives and works in the city for many years; he raises a family. Young adulthood turns to maturity and then to old age. Yet, although he had spends the vast majority of his life in the great city, he still does not find the meaning of life.

Thus, as an old man he continues his search. He leaves the city, walks for a long time, and comes upon a river. It is the same river that he and his best friend crossed so many years ago, when they first left their home village. The river is still wide and vast; it is still empty. But now Siddhartha looks at the river with new eyes. He realizes that he has spent his whole life trying to find the meaning of life by filling himself up. Now as an old man he comes to the knowledge that the meaning of life has been before him, wherever he was, all along. He only needed to empty himself sufficiently in order to find it.

Three days after the crucifixion Peter and John came to Jesus' tomb and were astonished to discover that the Lord's body was missing. Speaking of himself, St. John writes, "He saw and believed." (20:8b) What did John see and thus believe that day? He saw that the tomb was empty. He realized that his life was full and cluttered with many things. The question for him was, could he empty himself sufficiently to receive God, the Risen Lord?

We need to ask ourselves the same question. Can we see and believe or are our lives too cluttered to receive God? We are all busy people; we are addicted to many things. Some of us are addicted to work; some are addicted to school. Some people are addicted to pleasure. Some, unfortunately, are addicted to themselves. At times we are so busy that our priorities get messed up. Sometimes our addictions come ahead of our God. It cannot be this way, if we are to see and believe!

We might feel uncomfortable doing nothing, just being. It is difficult to accept the moment. However, if we empty ourselves somewhat then we can make room for God and God's works. The reality of Jesus' resurrection is a message of hope for our own resurrection. But our resurrection need not wait until our union with God in eternity. We can begin now by emptying ourselves. If we are empty enough, if we are open, then we have chosen, as St. Paul suggests in his Letter to the Colossians (3:1-4), the higher realm, that which comes from God. We will then be able to find God and in the process perform the works of the Lord—preaching, teaching, good works, and healing.

Jesus' resurrection asks us to revive the human spirit deep down inside each one of us. The empty tomb encourages us to empty ourselves sufficiently so we can be filled with God. Let us today be resurrected; let us empty ourselves. Let us be re-filled with the Lord, so that we too can see and believe!

Question: Is there room in my day to experience the unexpected presence of Christ?

Scripture Passage: "So if you consider me your partner, welcome him as you would welcome me." (Philemon 17)

Prayer: Jesus, help me to never allow your presence to pass me by.

Feeding Each Other

There is an ancient Asian tale which describes the difference between heaven and hell. The image of hell, so says the tale, begins with the description of a long banquet-like table around which many are seated preparing to eat. The meal is prepared by world-renowned chefs, abundant, and ready to be eaten. The glassware is Waterford Crystal and the dinnerware is the finest bone china. The tablecloths and napkins are made from the finest linen available. The scene is elegant and all seems normal except for the silverware; each utensil is three feet long. In observing the scene we see that nothing is happening; nobody is eating. In their attempts to eat, each person, because the utensils are so long, keeps bumping into the others. Tempers flare and chaos reigns. In the end, no one gets anything to eat.

The image of heaven begins with the same banquet table. The meal is prepared; the people are present. Again the silverware utensils are three feet long. All in heaven are eating, however. These people have learned that, because the silverware is so long, the only way they can eat is by feeding each other. Mutual cooperation allows all to be fed.

This Asian tale says something very powerfully about our modern world and society. It seems to say that individual pursuit will land us in the wrong place. The tale tells us about the differences between those who find total fulfillment and satisfaction in self, as opposed to those who find fulfillment and satisfaction in God. Our world places many temptations in our path. There is the temptation to self-indulgence from food, drink, or drugs. There is the temptation to total self-satisfaction in work or sport. There is also the temptation to complete self-reliance, the idea that we have no need for others. It is the mentality that says I can do it all myself. Such individual pursuit is the Asian image of hell.

Sacred Scripture speaks to us about the need to channel our efforts away from self and toward the one thing that is truly valuable in our lives, namely God. As described by St. Matthew (14:13-21), Jesus realizes that the people are hungry. But he also knows that their hunger is more than physical, it is one that has its roots in self-centeredness. The people have in certain important ways lost the true meaning of life. Jesus, in his efforts to feed the people, shows that their efforts must be channeled toward and centered in God. Jesus goes even further. To assure that any effort toward God should go unnoticed, all the fragments are gathered up so that no effort will be wasted.

The prophet Isaiah (55:1-3) tells the Hebrews that they spend money, time and effort on what fails to satisfy. Working for oneself can never fully satiate one's need for God. The words of Isaiah can be applied to us as well. We work hard for ourselves which is certainly necessary in this day and age. However, sometimes we lose our focus and in our own personal efforts we fail to see the needs of others; we fail to feed those around us. God is our only source of satisfaction; everything else is empty and incomplete. We spend so much time concerned with the temporary, that is ourselves, that we at times neglect the time that must be spent in our relationship with God. Let us not forget Isaiah's words, "Listen carefully to me, and eat what is good and delight yourselves in rich food." (55:2b)

We need to feed God, as God feeds us. We do this by feeding God's people. We feed others most profoundly by living lives of service and ministry, lives to which all the baptized are called.

We also feed others by learning how to better love, both God and God's people. In order to love others we must first know that God loves us. St. Paul makes it clear in his Letter to the Romans (8:35-39) that nothing can separate us from God's love, except ourselves, our own ignorance, impatience, and inattention.

It is essential in our efforts to feed others that we keep our priorities straight. God must be number one in our lives; we must never waver or deviate from this tradition. Family and loved ones must be our second priority. All other things, such as work, relaxation, personal achievement must be somewhere down the line. If personal achievement or work come before God, then we cannot be centered in him. Failure will be the result.

We need to get excited about God in our lives. We do this by going outside of ourselves in our efforts to help others, especially those most in need. Placing our own needs and desires behind those of others is something we are called to do in order to feed God. Certainly we need to be concerned about ourselves; in our society few will do it for us. But if we can channel our efforts so that all may benefit, then we experience a greater sense of community and faith and in the process God is fed.

We come to Mass each Sunday to be fed at the Table of the Lord. We need to leave our cares, our personal "baggage" at the front door in order to fully enter into the celebration, so that God can feed us. God's feeding us can in turn get us involved, aid us to discover greater faith, and feed God's people in the process. Let us take the Asian image of heaven seriously and feed each other in imitation of Jesus, the source of all that is good.

Question: Do I work for myself alone? Am I concerned about the needs of others?

Scripture Passage: "Here am I, the servant of the Lord; let it be done with me, according to your word." (Luke 1:38)

Prayer: Lord Jesus, help me to feed others as You feed us with your word and sacrament.

Life Comes From the Cross

Christie Brown was born to a large and poor Irish family. His father was a laborer; his mother worked at home, keeping house and being principally responsible for the rearing of the nine Brown children. Christie was different than all his brothers and sisters; he was handicapped. He had been diagnosed as an infant with multiple sclerosis, a severely crippling and deforming disease. Christie could not walk; he could not even crawl. His speech was limited to grunts and groans. Christie Brown lived in obscurity and ridicule. Neighbor children made light of his handicap. His family carried him around in a wheelbarrow because they were too poor to afford a wheelchair. Everyone thought he would amount to nothing, everyone that is except Christie himself.

Christie was determined to live a productive life. His triumph began in a simple way. One evening as he lay on the floor of the family home he began to scribble something in chalk on the cement with his left foot, the only part of his body which he could control. The family watched in amazement as Christie spelled out the word "Mother." All his family thought that he had comprehended virtually nothing all these years, but they were wrong; Christie Brown had communicated for the first time. Over time, with the aid of a teacher, Christie learned to type with the toes of his left foot. He also learned to paint and draw, again using his left foot. He learned how to speak, first a word or two, then sentences, and ultimately normal conversation. Christie Brown wrote an award winning autobiography; his drawings and paintings have been exhibited in many of the world's galleries. Christie Brown had a terrible handicap in life, but he turned his handicap, his cross, into a great triumph.

Learning to accept life and making the most of what is given to us is a great challenge. Matthew's Gospel (16:21-27) presents a contrast between one who can accept life's fate and one who cannot. After professing that Jesus is the Messiah, Peter refuses to accept the future as outlined by the Lord. Jesus must die, this is his cross figuratively and literally. Jesus must leave our world; Peter is not able to accept the Lord's future fate. Jesus tells Peter what is necessary. "If any want to become my followers, let them deny themselves and take up their cross and follow me. For those who want to save their life will lose it, and those who lose their life for my sake will find it. For what will it profit them if they gain the whole world but forfeit their life?" (16:24-26a) If you lose your life in the present existence, if you can give your life to the Gospel message, then everlasting life will be yours.

Like Peter, who could not understand, Jeremiah was a reluctant prophet. Everyone laughed at his message; they refused to listen. His message of violence and outrage brings the anger of people upon him. Jeremiah suffers through a great internal crisis and does not want to accept his role. Eventually, however, his apprehension and refusal to accept his fate passes. He says, "If I say, 'I will not mention him or speak any more in his name,' then within me there is something like a burning fire shut up in my bones; I am weary with holding it in, and I cannot." (20:9) God has convinced Jeremiah to accomplish the task which God planned for him. The prophet can no longer hold off God's presence. It is difficult, but Jeremiah accepts God's will and mission for his life.

We live in a world which unfortunately gives us many crosses, but our cross can, like Jesus, become our triumph. Maybe your cross, like Christie Brown, comes in the form of a health problem, either personal or that of a loved one. Possibly your cross is a problematic situation in the family; possibly the cross you bear is a difficult work environment. We must do our best to help ourselves and others, but we must never surrender to life, throw in the towel, and give up. Rather, we need to take the life we have been given and make the most of it. Learning to transform pain into joy, defeat into victory, a reversal in life into a victory—this is the Christian calling.

Maybe the cross you bear is a relationship that is either strained or broken. We ask ourselves in such situations, where can the good be found; how can we grow from such difficult situations? We wonder where is the hand of God in such a cross; where can we go from here? Despite the pain of such a cross, God from the depth of our despair raises up people and situations which bring new meaning to a seemingly unmanageable situation. We must be open to God and allow him to work when relationships die.

Maybe the cross we bear is found in the general pressures of society, the pressure to give into what the world sees as important and in the process shut out God. Society says wealth, power and prestige are important. Our cross may be to stand against such attitudes, to buck the system and show another, more Christian way of looking at things. Possibly we are called, as St. Paul suggests (Romans 12:2) to a renewal of mind emphasizing Christian values and beliefs. We may become outcasts with some co-workers and friends because of our stand; we might suffer ridicule. But Jesus says, what does it profit a person to gain the whole world and ruin himself in the process.

Let us today pick up the cross of our life and follow Jesus. The cross might be heavy; it might be light. One thing is certain the cross exists in different ways for all. Let us deny ourselves in serving others. Let the cross of Christ encourage us to find hope and life in leading lives of holiness drawing ourselves and others closer to God.

Question: Do I run from the crosses of life or find ways to grow from them?

Scripture Passage: "For the message of the cross is foolishness to those who are perishing, but to us who are bing saved it is the power of God." (I Corinthians 1:18)

Prayer: Loving God, help me to see the cross as an opportunity to grow closer to you.

Getting Involved With God

Willy Loman lived in a world of indifference, a world where nobody seemed to care. Willy was a traveling salesman and not a very good one. He had been on the road for years going from town to town, selling one product after the other. After so many years of being on the road, Willy was tired. He told his boss he no longer wanted to travel. After all Willy was now 63 years old. He wanted to have a desk job in the office; the road and sales were for younger people. But Willy's boss would not listen. The boss said that Willy was a road man; this was his expertise. If Willy did not want to continue on the road then he would be let go. And so it happened, Willy was discharged from his position after a lifetime of service.

The reaction of Willy's family was not what most might expect. His wife and children were very cold to him. Willy's wife told him not to worry, that all would be well; he would eventually find another job. Her answer to her husband's dilemma was to get mad at the boss who had dealt him such a blow of injustice. She was not willing to help; she was not willing to listen. Willy's sons had a similar attitude. The boys were involved in their own lives; they could not stop long enough to feel the pain of their father and offer assistance.

Eventually Willy Loman died, a broken man. He did not die from disease or an accident; Willy Loman died from complacency. The lack of love, the indifference of those around him caused him more pain than the loss of his job ever could. Nobody seemed to care.

The world of Willy Loman, the attitude of indifference described in Arthur Miller's famous stage play, "The Death of a Salesman," is challenged by the lessons of Scripture. St. Luke's parable of the rich man (known traditionally as Dives) and Lazarus (16:19-31) gives us much food for thought. The rich man lives in a world of indifference; he does not see what is happening around him. He has not done anything wrong, at least nothing of an outward nature. We cannot say that he was a great sinner; we cannot say that he used his wealth in an unwise manner. We cannot even say that the rich man did not help Lazarus; he did allow him to eat the scraps from his table. The rich man, however, was complacent; he lived in a world of indifference. It did not matter to him that Lazarus was poor; he certainly could have done more. This same situation is described by the prophet Amos (6:1-7). People of his day lived without a care, ate and drank, and generally did not notice what was happening around them. They loved passively without any involvement; they chose to do only the minimum.

Christianity challenges, even commands us to get involved, to be people of action. Christianity by its very nature is action oriented. From the call received through baptism we have the responsibility to be people of service and commitment in caring out the dictates and commands of the Lord. Most people are good; very few people I think are bad. We are pretty good at meeting and fulfilling our commitments—to family, friends and those with whom we work. But our Christian vocation calls us to do more. Why? Because there are two types of sin, sins of commission and sins of omission. We cannot be complacent and feel we have done all that God asks of us.

We are called to action. How many times have we heard one say, "I don't want to get involved." We hear such words spoken concerning criminal activity, community relations, and even the

Church. How many times have you heard or maybe even said yourself, "I'm not going to vote—the issues are unimportant, the candidates don't impress me?" How many times have you been asked to help and said to yourself, "That is for others, not for me?" Such typical responses are the world of indifference, the world of Willy Loman. Our Christian commitment calls us to greater heights, to overcome such complacency, and to be people of action.

We can act; it is up to us. We can take notice of those around us—the poor, the unloved, those who live on the margins of mainstream society. We can get involved with our community; we can vote and be counted. We can show people we care by what we say and especially by what we do. We may worry about what our response should be. Will it be correct; what should I do? Our fears are real, but acting in a Christian manner most certainly is better than the complacency of inaction.

Willy Loman's family treated him with indifference. They could not take the time which was necessary to respond to his needs. He died alone, a broken man crushed by the callous and indifferent attitudes of others. Let us escape our credit card mentality which says buy now and pay later. Let us get involved today and in the process find the presence of God all around us.

Question: Do I choose to get involved or does my passivity say, "I don't care?"

Scripture Passage: "Truly I tell you, just as you did it to one of the least of these who are members of my family, you did it to me." (Matthew 25:40)

Prayer: Father, let me never be deaf to the cries of the needy or blind to acts of injustice.

God Can Complete Mission Impossible

It is 10PM, the children are in bed, school lunches are ready for tomorrow, and finally a half-hour of peace is found to watch the early news before bed. In less than eight hours it will be time to wake and begin another hectic day. This scene is all too familiar to families today. Parents rise early, prepare themselves for work, wake their children, make breakfast for all, grab a cup of coffee for the road, and head out to meet the snarl of traffic or the crush on the subway on the way to their jobs. Eight-hours on the job, coupled with commute time makes for a long work day, but our activities are hardly over when we return home. Dinner must be prepared, children need to be ferried to sports, music lessons, and libraries; civic and Church-related activities take us away from home. Family members often see each other as ships passing in the night; a family dinner with all present is a rare event. Life, which is so fast-paced, requires great commitments of time, and is often experienced with disappointment and pain, can easily discourage us; we might think life is "mission impossible."

Life today is a struggle which, with the passing of time, only seems to become more complex. Difficult tasks in life, what we might perceive to be impossible missions are the reality of our daily life. However, lest we lose hope, we must realize that throughout salvation history God has sent people on what must have seemed impossible missions, but they always went with the tools needed to successfully complete the task.

In the Book of Genesis we are introduced to Abram, who we know better know by his more familiar name of Abraham. He was a wandering Semite who lived in a region east of the Jordan River. At the time Abram did not know God, but God nevertheless called him for an important and difficult mission. Abram was asked to leave his kinsfolk and his father's house. In other words, God asked him to dissociate himself from his pagan past. But God asked more when Abram, who was an old man, was told to follow this unknown God to a foreign land. Abram, however, did not travel alone; he had God's covenant and favor with him. God promised that Abram would be the father of a great nation, that all people would respect him. God told Abram that all the communities of the earth would find a blessing in him. Abram accepted God's mission, a rather amazing feat considering the circumstances. Abram's act of obedience might have seemed to him to be mission impossible in leaving all that he knew and loved behind and traveling to a foreign land. Yet, he undertook the mission and in the process initiated God's plan of salvation history.

Moses may have had the greatest challenge in his mission to lead the Hebrews out of bondage in Egypt. Moses did not feel adequate for the mission; he often confessed to God that he was not a man of speech. Yet, God gave him his brother, Aaron, to speak for him, sent a series of ten plagues to convince Pharaoh of God's commitment to the Hebrews, and provided him with the gifts of leadership to accomplish his goal. The repeated faithlessness and constant complaints of the Israelites became a heavy burden for Moses and he often asked to be relieved of his role as liberator and leader. But whenever the task seemed impossible God provided what was needed—manna and quail for food, water from a rock to drink, and the bestowal of God's spirit on elders to share the burdens and responsibilities of leadership.

Throughout the Hebrew Scriptures there are numerous other references to those who carried out impossible missions with the help of God. Samson defeated the Philistines, David slew Goliath, Solomon built the Temple, Jonah converted the Ninevites, and the great prophets such as Isaiah, Jeremiah, and Ezekiel fearlessly spoke God's word to unsympathetic, disinterested, and even hostile crowds. In each case God provided the assistance, words, or actions needed to complete what may have appeared at the time to be mission impossible.

Jesus also had an important mission on earth, one that he at times might have thought to be mission impossible. He was asked to convert his fellow Jews to a new and higher understanding of God. Jesus was asked to gather all people and tell them that henceforth God's loving plan was for all people for all time. In order to carry out this difficult mission it was necessary that Jesus be recognized as God. Although many events narrated in the New Testament, especially the miracle stories, testify to Christ's divinity, the story of Jesus' Transfiguration demonstrated most profoundly how Jesus was recognized as God in two important, fundamental, yet different ways. First, the event itself manifested God's presence. Jesus' face became radiant and his clothes were made dazzlingly white. The Lord is heard in conversation with Moses and Elijah. Only God could be so manifest. If, however, that was not enough evidence for those who witnessed the event, Peter, James, and John, God the Father speaks from the heavens, "This is my Son, the beloved; with him I am well pleased; listen to him." (Matthew 17:5b)

For those with eyes of faith it was clear that Jesus was God, but the Lord's mission was made no easier by this revelation. I am certain in his human nature Jesus must at times have believed that his task was mission impossible. He was accepted by very few; many of those who followed him could not understand his teaching. He was betrayed by one of his inner circle and was denied three times by the one whom Jesus himself hand-picked to be his earthly successor. Yet, through it all, Jesus' life and most especially his passion, death, and resurrection brought salvation history, initiated by the obedience of Abram, to its climax. Jesus' redemptive act of love on the cross brought the possibility of salvation to all people for all time. Jesus completed his mission impossible.

We will face many difficult challenges in our lives, tasks that may seem to be impossible missions. In the journey of our working days we will face some trying situations. We may face obstacles that will not allow us to work as we want. Coercion, threat or the temptation of reward may "force" us to do things in a manner which we know might hurt or ill-effect another. We may be required to relocate in order to stay with the company or worse still our job might be lost. At such times we wonder what we will do and what the future will hold. Families experience many difficult challenges. Some people are asked to walk the road of ill-health with a spouse, child, sister, brother, or another relative. Tough love may be required in our relationship with one who suffers from addiction. Many people must suffer the pain of observing a loved one reject God and the Church and opt for the things of the world. All of us will one day face the death of one close to us. The Church will also bring us challenges. We pray fervently to God for our needs, yet our prayers are not answered in the way or time that we want; we might even feel

God has abandoned us. Sometimes we lose sight of the road; we move off the track or even reverse course in our journey to God.

We will experience difficult times in our life, with our jobs, our families, and the Church, challenges which may seem to be impossible missions. But if we, like Abram, Moses, the prophets, and Jesus, can persevere and continue on the road, then God will recognize and reward our efforts. The task will not be easy; the road to God has pitfalls and obstacles. St. Paul advised his friend Timothy of this reality, "Do not be ashamed, then, of the testimony about our Lord or of me his prisoner, but join with me in suffering for the gospel." (II Timothy 1:8) But he also assured him, "If we have died with him we will also live with him; if we endure we will also reign with him." (II Timothy 2:11-12)

We must constantly re-evaluate our lives and renew our determination to walk the journey of life which one day will lead to union with God. It will not be an easy journey, if taken seriously, but it is the only path that will one day lead to eternal life. Let us, therefore, walk the road; let us take on what seems to be mission impossible. God will strengthen us, reward our efforts, and use us to complete his work on earth. Our reward in heaven will be great.

Question: How often have I given up on projects simply because the task seemed to difficult or even "mission impossible?"

Scripture Passage: "Proclaim the message; be persistent whether the time is favorable or unfavorable; convince, rebuke, and encourage with the utmost patience in teaching." (II Timothy 4:2)

Prayer: Jesus, grant me the grace of perseverance in all my endeavors.

Responsibility is a Privilege

Two strangers, bright and capable women, appeared one day in a small rural community. It was the Advent season; Christmas was just around the corner. This particular community was in search of its identity; it was looking for its role in God's overall plan of salvation. Like many communities this town had its problems. Some of these difficulties were readily observable while others were more deep-seeded and difficult.

The physical problems centered themselves around an annual Christmas pageant, a combination of music, word, and theater, all performed to re-create the events of Bethlehem 2000 years earlier. The choir of angels was anything but angelic, the acting was poor, and the church organ rivaled the choir for its production of off-key notes. The non-observable problems were more difficult. The townspeople were unable to accept God's action in their lives. A little girl was plagued by a virus which had attacked her heart and would soon claim her life. People felt God was unfair to allow such a situation to develop. Two brothers were unable to live together, the older caring for and taking responsibility for the younger who was mentally handicapped. The care giver was angry at God for burdening him with such a responsibility. The two strangers aimed to unite the community and show them a way to find God's plan.

One of the women worked to solve the physical and more observable problems. She organized the pageant, rehearsed the choir, and even managed to repair the organ. The other visitor aimed to show the people that acceptance was necessary in their lives; they needed to believe in the active presence of God. Complaints continued to spew forth from people's lips; the anger and inability to grow continued. One day, however, in a fit of frustration herself, the stranger told the brother care giver, "Responsibility is not a burden given by God, it is a privilege."

The words stung the man and he began to see other possibilities in his life. Conversion and transformation began to occur and he once again began to love God and his brother. In the end the pageant was a success, the brothers were reconciled, the little girl was taken by God to heaven, and the townspeople came to realize that their visitors were actually God's messengers, the angels. The people learned that responsibility and privilege are not opposite ends of the spectrum or antithetical; they are, rather, complementary in helping us build God's kingdom on earth.

Mary of Nazareth was a woman who lived a life of privilege. She was the Mother of God, in Greek the *Theotokos*, a term first proclaimed at the Council of Ephesus in 431. The birth of Jesus, was, however, preceded by another great privilege in her life, her Immaculate Conception. When Mary's earthly life was over she was again granted the great privilege of not experiencing the corruption of the grave through her assumption, body and soul into heaven. This life of privilege was, however, not lived in isolation. Rather Mary's role was one of sorrow and pain; her lot was a spiritual martyrdom as painful in many ways as the cross of her Son. Simeon's prophecy at the presentation of Jesus (Luke 2:34-35), that a sword would pierce the heart of Mary, told her from the outset that her privilege as Mother of God would be played out in pain. The manifestation of this journey came very soon as the Holy Family was exiled to Egypt to escape the clutches of King Herod. It was Mary who walked the Via Dolorosa or Way of Sorrow, stood beneath the cross, and held the lifeless body of Jesus, her only Son, in her arms.

Mary's life of privilege and responsibility must have caused her to reflect, as St. Luke (2:16-21) about God's active presence in her life. She must have believed as the author of the Book of Numbers (6:22-27) says that God had blessed all Israel. Only through Mary's belief in the active presence of God could she have carried her cross of pain. She had many burdens. But she never flinched, never hesitated or asked, "Why?" Rather, she accepted her role and showed that all responsibility, even that of being the sorrowful mother, is a form of privilege. Because of this, as she proclaims in her famous prayer of thanksgiving, the Magnificat, "Surely, from now on all generations will call me blessed." (Luke 1:48b)

We need to emulate Mary and her ability to transform difficulty, challenge, and pain into privilege. We have been privileged in many ways. St. Paul (Galatians 4:4-7) speaks of one of our common privileges, that of being children of God. God created us, chose us, and now sends us forth to continue the work of salvation. God has also released us from the bonds of slavery; we enjoy another great privilege of freedom. But, like the people of that small town discovered and the life of Mary demonstrates, responsibility accompanies privilege. We all have responsibilities and I suspect if we were honest many times we wish we didn't have some of them. At work we are responsible for a project which weighs us down. Family responsibilities sometimes create a burden which we would like to lighten. The community and the Church also call us to tasks and responsibilities that at times overwhelm us. But we are challenged by God's word and the life of Mary, the Mother of God, to take a new look, to find hope and privilege in a sea of difficulty and challenge. The solution to the difficulty is not the elimination of problems, but rather the acceptance of the cross.

Thomas Moore in his popular 1992 book, *Care of the Soul*, speaks of transforming the difficult and challenging into useful and growth-filled experiences. It is not easy, but then life and Christianity were never meant to be a bed of roses. Let us, therefore, reflect upon the challenges and responsibilities of our lives. Let us, like Mary, grasp the opportunity, accept the cross, and discover the privilege present therein. May we "seize the day," in Latin *Carpe Diem*. Who knows, by such action, as the author of the Letter to the Hebrews (13:2) has expressed it, we may entertain angels without knowing it.

Question: Do I see the responsibilities of life as opportunities for growth?

Scripture Passage: "The Lord said to Cain. 'Where is you brother Abel?' He said, 'I do not know; am I my brother's keeper?'"(Genesis 4:9)

Prayer: Father, help me to always fulfill the responsibilities you give to me.

Agape: The Highest Form of Love

In the mid 1960s, there was a popular song on the radio, "Love Is Just a Four-Letter Word." The song was composed and sung by Joan Baez, a well-known folk singer of the period. In the lyrics of the song, Ms. Baez tried to show that love, although it has only four letters, and therefore, might be thought by some to a simple word, because it is so short, is in reality a very complex concept. The experience of life tells us that she is right; love is a very involved idea.

The ancient Greeks, a very intelligent and civilized people, also realized that love was a complicated idea. Among the many gifts that the Greeks gave us was the study of philosophy, the science of thought. In this discipline the Greeks used three different words to adequately express the concept of love, knowing it to be a broad idea. The first type of love for the Greeks was *phileo*. This is brotherly and sisterly love. It is the type of love expressed between siblings, the love shared with a best friend. This is certainly a special form of love that is widely observed in our world. The second word the Greeks used to express love was *eros*. This is romantic love, the love between one man and one woman. This type of love is centered in self. Although we may give much to the one we love in such a way, *eros* is an emotion which is self-satisfying, a personal need that all people feel and desire. The third form, and for the Greeks the highest form of love, is *agapao*, commonly known as agape. This is the love we outwardly express in our service, ministry, and relations with others. Agape is centered on the other, not the self. It is, therefore, a special and powerful love which is rooted in the Christian understanding of faith and Jesus' message of love and service. This special love is expressed in relationships, in families and between best friends, where sacrifice and mutual respect are paramount.

Scripture, best represented by the entire corpus of St. John's works in the New Testament, is filled with the idea of love, specifically God's love for us. We remember the famous line in John's Gospel, "For God so loved the world that he gave his only Son, so that everyone who believes in him may not perish but may have eternal life." (3:16) The first epistle of John also describes God's love. It was the love of God for us that allowed Jesus to be like one of us in all things, save sin. Jesus not only took on our humanity, He chose to willingly die that we might have life. This is the supreme sacrifice, this is love, this is agape. But John also says, "Beloved, since God loved us so much, we also ought to love one another." (I John 4:11) We probably will not be called upon to physically die for another, but there is much dying to others that can be accomplished along the road of life as we journey to the Father.

The other aspect of agape which Scripture describes is mutual respect. St. Luke's description of Jesus being "lost" in Jerusalem forces us to place our feet in the shoes of Mary and Joseph. The Jewish people each year at the time of Passover would make a pilgrimage to the holy city of Jerusalem. As good Jews of faithful practice the Holy Family journeyed to Jerusalem, along with their friends and relatives, to celebrate the Passover feast. As they begin their return trip to Nazareth, Mary and Joseph quite logically assumed that Jesus was in their party; where else would he be? But after one day's travel he is not found in the party. As any loving couple would do, Mary and Joseph rush back to Jerusalem to find their Son. If you have seen the movie "Home Alone II," then I am sure that Mary and Joseph felt just like that family whose little boy was all alone in the big city of New York. Joseph and Mary searched frantically for Jesus and on the third day they finally found him. What was Mary's reaction? It was certainly what you might expect, " Child, why have you treated us like this? Look, your father and I have been searching for you in great anxiety." What is Jesus' response? It wasn't what you might expect, "Why were you searching for me? Did you not know that I must be in my Father's house?" (2:48b-49)

Mary and Joseph did not understand the response of Jesus. Herein, however, lies the great lesson. Although Mary and Joseph do not understand Jesus' action, they, nevertheless, have sufficient respect for him that they do not question him further. They realize that Jesus must do what he must do. Jesus, in turn, shows respect for his mother and foster-father. As St. Luke says, "Then he went down with them and came to Nazareth, and was obedient to them." (2:51a).

Families must celebrate their special relationships—between spouses, parents and children, and siblings. We have seen that such love is best expressed in agape, that is sacrifice and mutual respect. Parents sacrifice for their children in many ways. Parents sacrifice their time, their energy, their resources and even at times their own hopes and desires so that their children may prosper a little more. When there comes a conflict between the needs of parent and child, the good parent will often defer to the needs of the child. Although children are for the most part on the receiving end of sacrifice, they too can sacrifice in many beautiful and significant ways. Children can sacrifice some of their time and energy to help out a little more around the house, beyond what is ordinarily expected, such as watching a baby brother or sister when Mom and Dad are occupied. Children can also sacrifice by helping others, especially relatives, neighbors, and friends who might need a little extra help in some area.

Agape also means mutual respect. Children are raised to respect their elders. That is the way most people are taught. Parents serve and critique their children because they love them and because they believe direction and needed correction will make them better people in the end. Children do not always understand the methods or reasons of parents, but children should show respect for their parents and others, such as teachers, who are placed over them. Parents are usually on the receiving end of respect, but that does not mean that they too must show respect for their children. Showing respect means knowing when to back off in encouraging the individuality, uniqueness, and special needs of a child. This is many times difficult, but is necessary for mutual respect, love, and thus agape to flourish.

Let us take a lesson from the Greeks and from Sacred Scripture to better express our love for others through sacrifice and mutual respect. Let us follow the Master, Jesus our brother, friend, and Lord as we walk the journey of faith this day!

Question: How far am I willing to go in the service of others and demonstrate my love for them?

Scripture Passage: No one has greater love than this, to lay down one's life for one's friends." (John 15:13)

Prayer: Lord Jesus, help me to follow your example and love others as your Father loves all.

Section III
The Presence of God in the World

Introduction

Many years ago while serving as associate pastor of a parish west of Phoenix, Arizona I went to the church office early one morning to complete some work before the morning Mass. While I was there the phone rang. The local hospital was calling for me. A woman in the parish had just given birth and the new mother asked that I come to visit her. I knew the woman and her family rather well, but I also realized that her pregnancy had been quite difficult, so this was great and welcome news. I dropped my work, got into the car and made the short 15 minute drive to the hospital. When I arrived in the woman's room I saw her with her new son all wrapped in a blanket. Mother and child, who had been together for nine months were now with each other in a new way. The event for me was highly emotional. I felt the overpowering presence of God in what I saw. Only minutes before this little boy had been a great promise waiting to join our world; now he had arrived and his mother and I rejoiced. Clearly, this was the active presence of God in my friend's life and mine as well.

God is present in so many ways it is impossible to articulate all of them, yet often we fail to recognize the Lord's presence. When we slow down sufficiently from the terribly busy lives we lead we find God in many places. God is present in the beauty of the morning sunrise and evening sunset. The Lord is found in the powerful force of hurricane force winds and driving rain, but God is equally present in the beauty of a winter snow that gently falls from the sky or a cooling summer breeze that refreshes our weariness. God is most active and present in people, those with whom we share our lives closely on a daily basis and those we know only peripherally or not at all. The great challenge is to always look for and perceive the active presence of God, even when events and situations at times crash down upon us and one wonders if God is even concerned about our world. Yes, at times we become frustrated and begin to question the active presence of God, but we can easily be brought back to the reality of God's abiding presence with us when reflecting on events as ordinary yet as profound as the birth of a child, or the portents of sea and sky . We simply must make the time and not allow God to pass us by.

The reflections in this section describe how God is present in our world, both the obvious, and less discernible but nonetheless active manifestations. We know God is present for we daily feel the guiding hand of the Lord directing us along the proper path. We must learn our need to always listen to God and to trust that he will never lead us astray. Additionally, we must come to believe that God will always provide what we need and that the Lord's power can conquer any and all adversaries, but we must be ready and open to God's active presence.

God is actively present in our world and desires to share his life and joy with all of us, who, we must remember, are made in the Lord's image and likeness. Let us, therefore, open our eyes, ears, and minds to the possibilities of God's presence—today and always. If we can then God will enter us, we will become the physical presence of God in the world, and when God calls us we will hear, "Come, you that are blessed by my Father, inherit the kingdom prepared for you from the foundation of the world." (Matthew 25:34)

Advocates for the Body of Christ

Democracy, the hallmark and apex of contemporary government and political structures, provides many great privileges for those so governed. Citizens in democratic nations have the right of freedom of expression and action, within the dictates of the law; they have the right of due process and redress. Probably the greatest privilege that comes to those governed democratically is the right to vote. Through the ballot we elect our representatives who become our advocates in national, state, and local legislative bodies. Although recent apathy toward voting is a sad commentary on our nation and its democratic process, nonetheless those eligible to vote have advocates for their needs and causes. The Christian call, like the democratic process mandates that we be advocates for the message of Christ in our world. We must recognize Jesus' presence and then act on his behalf.

One contemporary uncanonized "saint" who recognized Jesus in others and became their advocate was Dorothy Day, who often said, "When I see the face of the poor, I see the face of Christ." Most people today are familiar with this great woman of faith and her advocacy for those with little or no voice in society. Born in 1897 in New York, she moved about frequently as a child because her father, a newspaper sports reporter, could not find stable employment. After several years the Day family settled in Chicago when her father secured a permanent position with the *Chicago Inter-Ocean*. Dorothy was gifted, like her father, with the ability to write and she parlayed that skill into a scholarship to the University of Illinois. However, she was bored at school; the regimen of classes and assignments was not for this woman who needed a cause. Initially her cause was radicalism. She quit school, moved back to her place of birth, and took up the cause of radical elements who were prevalent in New York in the period immediately after World War I. She associated freely with the Greenwich Village set, often listening to poetry recited by the famous playwright Eugene O'Neill. Her lifestyle was rather wild, including a common law marriage and an abortion. But, as she describes in her famous autobiography, *The Long Loneliness*, the birth of her daughter, Tamar Theresa, and the need for this child to have stability in her life, turned Dorothy to organized religion, and specifically to Catholicism.

Dorothy's religious background was sketchy at best. She was baptized as a child in the Episcopalian tradition but seldom practiced the faith. She saw in Catholicism the stability that had eluded her and what she believed was necessary for her daughter. Her conversion to the Church remains somewhat mysterious, but what she did with her new found faith is legendary, becoming the principle source of inspiration for two generations of Catholics and other Christians who find their purpose in the promotion of the social gospel message of Christ. Dorothy had her faith, but she needed a way to express it. That road was shown to her in December 1932 when, after praying for guidance at the National Shrine of the Immaculate Conception in Washington, D.C., where she had gone to cover a hunger march for *Commonweal* Magazine, she met Peter Maurin, a French émigré to the United States who had many ideas for social renewal, but needed a person like Dorothy Day to publicize his thought. Together they founded the Catholic Worker Movement in 1933 and its even today popular organ,

The Catholic Worker monthly newspaper, which is still sold for one cent.

Dorothy Day's ability to seek and find the face of Christ in the poor and her advocacy for those on the margins of society is best illustrated in one story, an incident that brought about the first house of hospitality. Dorothy had become an advocate for the poor and was running the newspaper from her own apartment. If space was available those without shelter were welcome. One day two women came and said they needed a place for the night, but Dorothy, looking about, told them, "You can see we have no room." The women left dejectedly, but a few days later one returned and, thus, Dorothy asked, "What happened to your friend?" The answer came, "She died the other night on the streets. She was despondent and threw herself under a train." The words struck Dorothy so powerfully that she immediately emptied the cash box, used for her own rent and needs, walked down the street, and rented a flat. The first house of hospitality was thus established. Dorothy Day looked in the eyes of the poor, saw Christ, and then became their advocate.

Recognizing the face of Christ in the poor and those who have little or no voice in society has been a great challenge since the dawn of Christianity. The apostles and other disciples who walked in Jesus' footsteps even found it difficult to recognize the presence of Christ after the resurrection. Scripture provides several examples of this rather odd reality. Mary Magdalen initially thought Jesus was the gardener (John 20:11-18); the disciples on the road to Emmaus only recognized him in the action of breaking the bread (Luke 24:13-35). When Jesus appeared to the apostles they thought he was a ghost. Jesus chastised the apostles for their failure to recognize him: "Why are you frightened and why do doubts arise in your hearts. Look at my hands and my feet; see that it is I myself." (Luke 24:38-

39a) Eventually the apostles calmed down and expressed sheer joy and wonder because Jesus was alive. The disciples were asked to recognize Jesus in another light, a new way. Could it be the case that Jesus was not immediately recognizable because he wanted his followers to be able to recognize his face, his presence in others? It took some effort, it seems, but the disciples did recognize the presence of the resurrected Christ. But they did more—they acted on behalf of the one whom they recognized.

Peter is rather fearless as Luke portrays him in the Acts of the Apostles. This is certainly a change for the apostle, who in the Gospel accounts is generally characterized as one who never quite understands, berates Jesus when the Lord reveals his need to suffer and die, (Matthew 16:21-23; Mark 8:31-33) and ultimately denies him three times in his hour of greatest need. (Matthew 26:69-75; Mark 14:66-72; Luke 22:54-62; John 18:15-27) Now Peter, the appointed head of the apostles, courageously speaks out in Jesus' name. He has recognized the presence of Christ and now becomes his advocate by witnessing and preaching to others. He cures the crippled beggar in Jesus' name; he fearlessly proclaims Jesus as Messiah and Lord. He willingly suffers imprisonment and insult for the Lord. Peter boldly proclaimed, "This Jesus is the stone that was rejected by you, the builders; it has become the cornerstone. There is salvation in no one else, for there is no other name under heaven given mortals by which we must be saved." (Acts 4:11-12) Peter's speech, given in Solomon's Portico, demonstrates how the apostle's faith was transformed, raised to a higher level, by the resurrection of Christ. He was not cowed by the Jewish authorities but boldly proclaims that he acts in the name of Jesus Christ, the one whom the Jews crucified. Jesus was rejected by his own people, but he has become the cornerstone of the new way.

One of the great challenges of the Church today is to discover the face of Christ and become his advocate in the world. Christ is present in all things at all times, but our limited finite ability as humans only allows us to find Jesus at special moments. The need to be open to the presence of Christ is critical. Christ will come and knock on the door of our hearts. As the Book of Revelation (3:20) states it, "Listen! I am standing at the door, knocking: if you hear my voice and open the door, I will come in to you and eat with you, and you with me."

Once we recognize the presence of Christ we must actively seek to minister to him, to be pro-active in our advocacy for others. The form of the ministry will vary depending on the capability of the individual, opportunity, and vocation. For some, like Dorothy Day, the form will be direct service to the poor. We may serve in a soup kitchen, donate time at a homeless shelter, or lobby our elected legislators, our advocates, to not forget those whose voice is weak or silent. Some will recognize Christ and be his advocate in the classroom. Teachers in parochial schools must always seek to promote faith and learning so that the two are not separate or lost. Some will serve the day-to-day needs of God's people in some direct parochial work such as religious education directors, liturgy coordinators, and pastoral assistants. Most will serve God's people through our day-to-day jobs and responsibilities with our families. This could possibly be the most important means because we daily encounter many who need our assistance. Christ is equally present in all; we simply must see his face and act in his name.

To recognize the face of Christ and to act, speak, and witness on the Lord's behalf is not only the call of the priest, the religious, or the one who may work in a parish. Such people have no corner on the market. No, all people who bear the name Christian, who have the privilege to bear the image of the crucified, have the obligation to seek Christ and to serve. Whether our life vocation is the single life, marriage, or religious life, whether we work for IBM, the local school district, or a convenience store, the call is the same—to recognize Jesus in others and act on their behalf.

St. Teresa of Avila, the famous sixteenth-century Carmelite mystic and religious reformer, understood the need to recognize Christ and minister to him. It was done by being the presence of Christ to others, the call and task of every Christian. It is the call of the priest; it is the call of the Christian. She wrote, "Christ has body on earth, but yours, no hands, no feet but yours. Yours are the eyes with which Christ looks with compassion for the world. Christ has no body on earth but yours." May we who seek to be disciples of Jesus believe, profess and witness the same!

Question: Where do I look for the presence of Christ? Has my scope been too narrow in the past?

Scripture Passage: "For where two or three are gathered in my name, I am there among them." (Matthew 18:20)

Prayer: Lord Jesus, help me to find you in the events, opportunities and people I encounter this day.

Reliance Upon God

Sophocles, the famous Greek dramatist, graced the world with his many plays. His famous trilogy of "Oedipus Rex," "Oedipus at Colonnus," and "Antigone" is his greatest legacy. In this trilogy there is a famous section known as the "Riddle of the Sphinx." In order for Oedipus to gain entry to his desired destination he must solve this famous riddle. The passage is as follows: What has four legs in the morning, two legs in the afternoon, and three legs in the evening? The answer is a human being. In the morning, the first period of our life, we crawl; we need all fours, legs and arms, to move and get around. In the great middle or afternoon of our life we walk upright on two legs. In the twilight of our life we often need some assistance, such as a cane or a helping hand; we use three legs in this stage of our life.

The riddle of the sphinx tells us something powerful about our reliance on others. When we are infants we need the support of others. We are totally dependent as young children on others, for food, clothing, shelter, love, in short all our needs. As children we trust that all will be provided. We don't worry; our trust is absolute in those who care for us. When we are old enough to walk we begin to rely on ourselves. We venture out, just a little at first, but later with ever more bold steps. We try things for ourselves. As time goes on our ability to trust in others begins to wane. Life throws us curves; we get knocked down and kicked around. Our trust shifts to a more exclusive reliance on the tangible and visible things of our world. We begin to say that we need to do it ourselves; we cannot rely on others any longer. Others just might not come through for us! When we get older, when we need that third leg, we again begin to trust in others. We can no longer do everything that we once could do. We need the aid of other people, for the complex and sometimes even the simple everyday tasks of life.

Scripture, like the Riddle of the Sphinx, tells us something about relying on others, specifically our need to rely on God. The Genesis account of Abraham's test of faith with his son Isaac illustrates this point. Abraham was an adult; he could walk properly and speak for himself. Yet Abraham placed his total reliance, his total life in God's hands; he had complete faith. We recall how God told Abraham that he would be the father of a great nation. Isaac was Abraham and Sarah's only child, the fruit of their old age. God then asked Abraham to sacrifice his one chance for heritage. For three days Abraham and his son Isaac journeyed, yet Abraham's faith never wavered. He was always ready to do what God asks. In the end he received his reward as the father of a great nation. Still today Jews see Abraham as their father in faith.

In II Timothy 1:8-10 we hear about the obedience of Jesus to God the Father. Jesus was human, like you and me, yet his faith, unlike ours, never vacillated. Jesus was obedient to God to the point of death on the cross. Because of his obedience Jesus was exalted and has become for us the great intercessor to God. This is why many prayers in the Christian tradition invoke Christ as the one through whom we make our intercession. Jesus' reliance on God was complete and total.

Conversion is necessary if we are to rely totally on the Lord. In the story of the Transfiguration (Matthew 17:1-9, Mark 9:2-8, Luke 9:28-36) Jesus is changed in appearance, but this transformation is temporary. The more important conversion is found with the apostles. Peter, James, and John are always there, it seems, when important events happen in the life of the Church. These men are the ones who are converted on the inside, where it counts and is permanent. Their conversion is to a life of total reliance on God. Certainly the apostles failed; they had their problems. But their faith in and obedience to Jesus was now a part of their being; they were changed forever.

If we were asked upon whom or what do we rely, what would be our honest answer? Some would answer that they rely on the material things of this life. These things are tangible, useable, and reliable, at least so it seems; we know for certain they exist. Some people rely on others in their life, family, friends or associates. Some rely totally on themselves.

All of us to a lesser or greater extent need to be converted to a complete and unqualified reliance on God. Abraham relied on God and became the father of a great nation. Jesus relied on the Father and was exalted to glory. If we rely on God and have complete faith, then we too will find the rewards of God.

Let us follow the example of Abraham and Jesus. Let us not be dominated by the world, as the Riddle of the Sphinx suggests. Let us hope and pray that if the world placed us on trial for our faith and reliance on God there would be sufficient evidence to convict us!

Question: When adversity strikes or challenges arise, to whom or what do we turn for strength and answers?

Scripture Passage: "Trust in the Lord with all your heart, and do not rely on your own insight." (Proverbs 3:5)

Prayer: Lord Jesus, help me to always place my trust in you.

"Speak, Lord, Your Servant is Listening"

In his 1996 book, *Under God, Indivisible*, the eminent historian of American religion, Martin Marty, describes the cultural and religious forces in the United States, in the period 1941 to 1960, as acting in a centripetal motion to bring unity to the nation. During the years of World War II the American people in almost every respect were united against the common enemies of Germany and Japan. When the guns of war fell silent and the Cold War began, the common thread to hold together the fabric of American unity was the specter of Communism, held in check internationally through the containment policy of President Harry Truman and domestically through the polemics of individuals like Senator Joseph McCarthy and groups, such as The Minute Women of the USA, Inc., and the John Birch Society. During the administration of President Dwight Eisenhower, a period where the United States reigned supreme, politically and economically, the fragile American unity was held together through a religious revival.

While World War II and the Cold War provided convenient international agents against whom all major religions could unite, the period of the 1950s became an opportunity for those gifted with words, either orally or in writing, to raise the religious conscience of the nation, and thereby, create an environment of religious revival, where the practice and acceptability of religion reached an all-time high, especially for Roman Catholics.

The most visible expression of this new religious frenzy was the promulgation of God's word, either through preaching or writing. The Trappist monk and convert to Catholicism, Thomas Merton, became an almost overnight sensation in 1948 with the publication of his autobiography, *The Seven Storey Mountain*. Merton's book provided answers to the perennial Protestant charge that Catholics were outsiders by providing an intellectual method of demonstrating the compatibility of Catholicism and American life. Norman Vincent Peale capitalized on the United States' premier international status in advocating that Americans should celebrate what they had accomplished. His 1950 monograph, *The Power of Positive Thinking*, transformed minds and became an almost instantaneous bestseller.

Bishop Fulton Sheen, who had gained national attention in 1930 as the premier and best-known speaker on NBC radio's, "The Catholic Hour," and had gained many followers through his voluminous writings, became a television sensation between 1952 and 1957 with his popular program, "Life is Worth Living." Sheen, who rivaled Milton Berle as the most popular television personality of the decade, captivated audiences by his ability to expound, seemingly effortlessly, on various topics, without any aides save a chalkboard and his "little angel," who magically erased the board as he wandered about the production set. Sheen's fame rose even more when people learned that his preparation for each show was fifteen minutes of meditation before the Blessed Sacrament. His message was Thomistic and held to traditional Catholicism, but few ever realized they were receiving a catechism lesson.

Billy Graham, the most significant evangelical preacher during America's religious revival of the 1950s, broadcast his message in stadiums and in the electronic media. Confidant of Presidents from Dwight Eisenhower forward, Graham successfully proclaimed the word to the American people in a way which, as Marty has suggested, brought greater unity to America's long-standing religious pluralism.

The message proclaimed by the likes of Merton, Peale, Sheen, and Graham brought greater religious cohesion to the United States, but this effect came about more because of the reaction of those who heard the message than from the message itself. Proclamations of the word, in whatever form they may take, are only as effective as is the ability of the receiver to "hear" and respond. While there is no doubt that the quality of a message and the competence of the person proclaiming it are vital, the message is of no use if it falls on deaf ears. If the audience to which a message is addressed is unwilling or unable to hear or read the word, understand it, and respond accordingly, then the missive has little value. Thus, it is clear that listening to God's word is of equal if not greater importance than its proclamation.

Scripture is filled with evidence of the efficacious preaching of Jesus of Nazareth. Crowds of people flocked to see him, to witness his miracles, and to hear him speak. The "Sermon on the Mount" (Matthew 5-7), the "Sermon on the Plain," (Luke 6:17-49), and the "Farewell Discourse of Jesus," (John 15-17) are only three of numerous references to the Lord's ability to attract attention by what he said. Yet, the attraction of his words only found meaning when those who heard his message or witnessed his actions were sufficiently inspired to tell others of the significance of what Jesus did and said.

How do we know that Jesus' listeners heard what he said? How can we measure the effectiveness of Jesus' words in their lives? One answer, simple though it may appear, is that we have the Scriptures and Christianity is one of the three great religious traditions of the Western world. If Jesus' message was not efficacious, if he was not able to convince people that his words had meaning for life, today and in the eternal life to come, than the world would not know of him. People would not have been inspired to write the books of the New Testament. Jesus' life would be a footnote in history and he could be classified with Theudas and Judas the Galilean (Acts 5:33-39) as a religious zealot whose followers dispersed upon his death. But Jesus' words were impressive; his actions were almost beyond belief. St. Mark's Gospel (1:21-27) provides an excellent example of how people reacted to Jesus:

They went to Capernaum; and when the Sabbath came, he entered the synagogue and taught. They were astounded at his teaching, for he taught them as one having authority and not as the scribes. Just then there was in the synagogue a man with an unclean spirit, and he cried out, "What have you to do with us, Jesus of Nazareth? Have you come to destroy us? I know who you are, the Holy One of God." But Jesus rebuked him, saying, "Be silent and come out of him!" And the unclean spirit, convulsing him and crying with a loud voice, came out of him. They were all amazed, and they kept asking one another, "What is this? A new teaching—with authority! He commands even unclean spirits, and they obey him."

Why does history remember St. Paul, Thomas Aquinas, Martin Luther, Dietrich Bonhoeffer, Dorothy Day, and Oscar Romero? All of these people spoke God's word in some way, but more importantly people listened to their words, observed their actions, and responded. People's lives were positively influenced because they took the time to listen to God's word as it was presented in its various ways. History remembers Jesus and thousands of others who in different ways proclaimed God's word, utilizing the wondrous gifts given them by the Creator. But the process of personal and communal transformation began when people heard or read the proclamation, digested it, and then used it to make a difference in their lives and the lives of others. The listeners and observers told others of their positive experience.

God's word is being proclaimed in various, multiple, and expanding ways in our ever-more technical society. In this new millennium, human society has the greatest opportunity in world history to encounter God's word, but if we are not listening, if we are not receptive, than the proclamation will be lost, and we as individuals and society as a whole will be the big losers. We need to make the commitment now to become better listeners.

While the active role of human communication is generally more satisfying, easier, and because of its simplicity less taxing than a passive mode, Scripture provides several important examples of the importance of the passive role in communication. After the prophet Elijah walked forty days and forty nights to the Mountain of God, Horeb, the Lord asked him to stand at the mouth of the cave to encounter God as he passed by. Like most people Elijah expected the Lord to be manifest is some powerful, highly visible or audible, or demonstrable way. Thus, Elijah was mystified when God was not found in the fire, the wind, or the great earthquake, but was discovered in a "sound of sheer silence." (I Kings 19:11-13a) The Hebrew Scriptures tell us of Samuel's first encounter with the Lord (I Samuel 3:1-10). The young man heard a voice calling him in his sleep, but he assumed it was his mentor, Eli. The experience and sage of the older man, however, told him that the subtle voice heard could only be that of the Lord. Thus, Eli tells young Samuel: "Go, lie down; and if he calls you, you shall say, 'Speak, Lord, for your servant is listening.'" Only when

Samuel was passive did he encounter God. It was his ability to listen that allowed God's message to enter, transform his life, and ultimately lead him to his role as prophet in Israel.

History records the great speeches, writings, and accomplishments of few, but it does so only because many more heard, read the words, or witnessed the accomplishments, told others, and were transformed. Each and every day of our lives is an opportunity to read, listen and observe, reflect, and be transformed. People of faith daily encounter God through prayer, but what is the content and matter of our prayer? Most people are very adept at vocalizing or for some writing prayers of praise, thanksgiving, and petition. When we need something we are not afraid to tell God. When the going gets tough and our needs seem to be magnified, we are generally good at expressing ourselves. The active element of prayer is essential; humans must tell God their needs, even though God is well aware of our thoughts and necessities. The main problem, however, is that our ability to listen to God's response is generally poor. Prayer is our daily conversation with God; it is our opportunity to be in close communication with our Creator, his Son, Jesus Christ, and their Holy Spirit. Prayer, like any good conversation, be it with family member, friend, colleague at work or neighbor next door, must be a two-way street. When we ask our spouse or friend for a favor or advice, we must listen to the response in order to gain that which we seek. Similarly, when we speak with God we need to listen to God's response. The answer seldom comes like a response in human conversation and it generally does not come with the rapidity of a bolt of lightening. Answers do come, however, and we must be passive enough in order to "listen" and recognize them. Eli's advise to his young protégé was solid. We, like Samuel, must say, "Speak, Lord, your servant is listening. You have the words of everlasting life."

In a world that demands performance measured by visible and tangible accomplishments, it is very difficult to be passive and wait for God's response. We always feel the need to do something, to be active, and thus demonstrate that we are useful. Some people will be active as the source of that which others receive. Most, however, play a passive role, listening to, reading about, and observing the world around us. But whichever role may predominate in our lives, all of us must develop the ability to listen. If we cannot listen we will never hear God's voice, our direction in life will be compromised, and we will never accomplish the mission that God gives us, as it is slowly but most assuredly revealed to us. We must make a special effort to avoid society's mandate for tangible results and strive to listen. As one wise nun once told me, "God gave us two ears and one mouth, so we should listen twice as much as we speak!"

Historians write of the accomplishments of famous people and how their efforts in some way were noteworthy. While no one would argue the need for competent people to lead in word and action, the reality is that the significance of words and actions is dictated by the response to them by the people to whom they are proclaimed or demonstrated. Fulton Sheen could have spoken on radio and conducted a weekly television show, but history would not recognize him if people were not attracted to and transformed by his words. In a similar way the accomplishments of Thomas Merton, Norman Vincent Peale, Billy Graham, and countless other people of historical significance would not be told today unless the listening and observations of the majority effected a positive change in the lives of individuals and society. Jesus, the Son of God and our Messiah, spoke forcefully and eloquently and performed miracles that could not even be imagined, but we know of his great words and works because countless millions have listened and been transformed. Let us, therefore, listen to God's word; let us observe closely God's action in the world. Let us engage our passive sense, as well as our active, using all our talents and gifts in a unity as we move along the path to God's reign and eternal life.

Question: How well do I listen to the needs of others, such as the cry of the poor and the pleas for justice in the world?

Scripture Passage: "Let anyone who has an ear listen to what the Spirit is saying to the churches." (Revelation 2:7)

Prayer: Lord, help me to open my ears to your call and respond with an unselfish heart.

Nothing is Too Difficult for God

In mathematics the concept of "Pi" is an example of a radical. It is a term which cannot be precisely or fully defined or known. We all learn in grade school that pi is 3.1416.... Pi cannot be fully known because it consists of an infinite string of numbers that come after the decimal point. Unlike the number 100 of even 50.50 which have definite and very precise values, pi is not totally definable.

Since pi is an infinite number we can only approximate its value. Some people have memorized the number pi to 200 places or more. One could memorize pi to 200 times 200 places and still have only an infinitesimal understanding of the number for infinity is forever. We who live a finite existence, can only understand something that has bounds. Thus, we make an approximation for pi and say it is good enough. We make a compromise; we cheat a bit. We use pi to calculate certain quantities that we need for building or designing some object. Our approximation is usually adequate for our needs.

Placing limits on things is the human reality. Humans can go only so far in understanding the infinite. We have never seen anything that is infinite and thus we can only guess at what infinity is. We know it is big, that is goes on forever. But this can lead to confusion, because we can only think on the finite level. When we place limits or boundaries on things it makes life more understandable, at least we can recognize that which we are trying to define.

God is infinite, that is what we have been taught since the time we first began to understand what others told us. The Hebrews believed that Yahweh was infinite, all powerful, all knowing, and omnipresent. Christians believe that Jesus is like the Father in all things and, therefore, is infinite. Jesus displayed compassion and love which were beyond human understanding.

Since God is infinite, how can we understand God? We make an attempt to understand God by placing limits on God. We set boundaries that God cannot exceed so as to make possible some understanding of the infinite. Theologically speaking, I suspect, there is a need to speak of God in some finite manner. Without some bounds God is unapproachable on an intellectual level.

Our propensity to place limits on the infinite can lead to problems, however, when we speak of our faith in God. Human beings for centuries have been placing restrictions, limits, and boundaries on their faith in God. The Hebrews were a people who constantly wanted a sign that God was with them in their struggles. They were never satisfied. God wrought the plagues in Egypt, parted the Red Sea, provided water and food in the desert, and made Israel victorious in battle when they claimed the promised land. Yet, the Hebrews continued to look for signs. The limits of their faith placed limits on their belief in God's providence. The stories of the judges and prophets of ancient Israel describe over and over again the people's inability to believe that God truly is infinite and will never abandon his greatest creation, the human race.

People in the time of Jesus also wanted signs. God was again placed in a straightjacket, tied up, and not allowed to be infinite. The limited faith shown by the Pharisees and other religious leaders of Jewish society was applied to their unbelief in Jesus. People were amazed each time Jesus performed something miraculous. It was only because people had little faith that the actions of an infinite God were so striking. As Jesus said to his followers, "If you had faith the size of a mustard seed, you could say to this mulberry tree, 'Be uprooted and planted in the sea' and it would obey you." (Luke 17:6)

People today are still placing limits on God. It is only natural; it is the only way we can know something of God. Yet, we transfer our limitations on the concept of God to our faith. We refuse to believe that God truly can do all things. We constantly need to be reminded of Jesus' words, "For God all things are possible." (Mark 10:27b)

To believe in the infinite is a great challenge. Christianity is such a belief. To speak of God as a person, to draw a picture of God or think of him standing before us is at best an approximation. It is the best we can do, however, and thus is important and useful. We cannot, however, hold such limitations on our faith and what God can do for us. God truly is infinite and thus capable of all things. When we speak with and listen to God in prayer, let us remember to keep the doors of possibility open. God knows our needs before we can even share them with him. Let us allow God's gift of faith to be boundless, infinite. If we can do this, then we can truly believe that nothing is impossible with God!

Question: Do I unconsciously limit God's ability to act in our world?

Scripture Passage: "Seek the Lord while he may be found, call upon him while he is near." (Isaiah 55:6)

Prayer: Father, open my mind and heart fully to experience your presence in all things.

God Is Our Permanent Hope

"Four score and seven years ago, our fathers brought forth on this continent a new nation conceived in liberty and dedicated to the proposition that all men are created equal." These words of President Abraham Lincoln at the dedication of the Gettysburg National Cemetery will always be remembered by students of American history. The year was 1863; the nation was in the midst of the great Civil War. After eighty-seven years of unity, the great house which was the union was divided. President Lincoln was familiar with the Bible. He must have read Mark 3:20-35, for he knew that a house divided could not stand.

Abraham Lincoln looked for what was permanent in the life of the nation. He looked for that which would last forever. For Lincoln it was the principle of democracy that would live forever. That is the reason he finished his famous "Gettysburg Address" with the words, "that government of the people, by the people, and for the people, shall not perish from the earth!"

Scripture provides a contrast between the permanent and the temporary, between the finite nature of humans and the infinite nature of God. In the Book of Genesis (3:9-15) we hear of the battle between God and Satan. Adam and Eve were fooled by Satan. They were looking for self-gratification; they were looking for a special knowledge. But what they wanted was only temporary; it would not last. God, however, the one who is permanent, defeats Satan. The serpent will forever crawl on his belly. Adam and Eve could not exist divided between God and Satan. Thus, God defeated the serpent so that the permanent would endure.

In the Gospel of Mark (3:20-35) Jesus is accused of having divided loyalties by belonging to Satan and doing his works. The Lord claims, however, that a house divided cannot stand. Although Satan fights against Jesus, the Lord is triumphant. The evil of Satan was temporary; it has now been vanquished. The permanent is God and God has triumphed. The essential message of Jesus' miracles and healing is that he is stronger than Satan. Satan has been bound, as the Gospel says, and Jesus has plundered his house.

We live in a world which is constantly in a battle between the temporary and the permanent. Most of our association with the world is of a temporary nature. Today's society is in many ways a throw-away world; everything is disposable. We have take out lunch and dinner, disposable plates, and throw-away razors. In many ways this reality has made life easier. In another way, however, such a manner of life is very misleading; it gives us a false impression of the good.

Our society is full of examples of how the temporary and the permanent vie for our attention and respect. One example is the law vs. faith. The law helps us now, but we cannot take it with us. The law is only a means to an end. Faith, on the other hand, lasts forever; it leads us to wholeness and goodness in our quest for God. Another example is fun vs. community. Everyone looks for and needs a certain amount of fun in their life; we need to entertain ourselves. If we are not cautious, however, fun can become a way of life for some of us. Fun is only temporary, it will not last long. Community, in contrast, leads to life. Community is a structure, it will not disappear or dissolve. A third example is friends and relationships vs. God. Friends come and go in our lives. We are lucky if we have three or four extra special friends throughout our lifetime. Relationships are important, even necessary, but they are present only in this life. God, however, lasts forever; God is the very reason for our life. Since God is the source of our life, all our efforts should be directed to returning to God. The law, fun, and friends are all good and help us to be whole, but in the end they are temporary; they do not last. Faith, community, and God, on the other hand, are permanent; they will bring us to salvation.

The history of the United States and its great Civil War proved the words of Jesus in Scripture to be true, a house divided cannot stand. The temporary is just that, it cannot long endure. We need more than the temporary in order to find our goal of union with God. Similarly Abraham Lincoln believed that the principles of equality and justice must endure, so that the nation might live and find's its true destiny in God's eyes as well.

Jesus defeated Satan and the permanent overcame the temporary. In our plastic, temporary world, let us look to the permanent, that which lasts. Let us look to our God for life now and salvation in the life to come!

Question: Do I seek temporary and readily available answers to life's questions or can I be patient for God's response?

Scripture Passage: "He alone is my rock and my salvation, my fortress; I shall not be shaken." (Psalm 62:6)

Prayer: Lord, help me to value more fully the things that have true meaning in life.

Jesus: A Spiritual Revolution

Once upon a time there was a beautiful queen who gave birth to a handsome baby boy. The King was, of course, elated about the birth of his son and so to honor the occasion he called in the royal gardener and revealed to him a plan for the future. The King was very wise and he realized that one day his newborn son would sit on his throne. As king he would choose the fairest, brightest, and most beautiful woman in the land to his wife and queen. To so honor his son and future daughter-in-law, the King commissioned the royal gardener to develop the most beautiful flower in the whole world. The gardener readily accepted the challenge for he had great respect for the King.

The gardener immediately set to work on his task. He chose the rose as he felt it was the most beautiful and regal of all flowers. The gardener worked for many months which turned into many years. He cross pollinated one plant to another and made all kinds of grafts. In the process he created all manner of blossoms and blooms, of all shapes, sizes, and colors. Many of the blossoms were beautiful, but none was adequate for the future queen. After all she would be the fairest, brightest, and most beautiful woman in the realm. The gardener continued with his work even when the king died in battle with a rival army.

The new young king did not marry for many years which gave the gardener more time to perfect his masterpiece. In the process he grew old and feeble. One day good news was broadcast throughout the realm, the king had chosen his bride and a wedding date had been set. The news came none too soon for the gardener had finally perfected his work. The rose he developed rivaled the heavens with its beauty. It was fine and delicate and mirrored all the colors of the outside world. The gardener called it the Rainbow Rose. Although it stood in the middle of the garden, among a myriad of flowers, the Rainbow Rose stood above them all, as the new queen would stand above all women in the realm. The gardener had done himself proud and honored the memory of the late king.

The day of the wedding the sun rose high in the sky; the weather was ideal. After the ceremony the royal couple strolled through the garden. To no surprise of the gardener the couple migrated almost immediately to the center of the garden where the Rainbow Rose was located. With her back to the gardener the young queen bent down and picked a blossom. "A royal rose for a royal lady," the gardener thought. But when the queen turned around the gardener was shocked for in the hands of the queen was not the Rainbow Rose, but a common ordinary red rose. The gardener was bewildered and angry; he did not understand. How could she choose a common rose over the beauty of the Rainbow Rose? He had to find the reason. The gardener approached closer to the royal couple. "My lady," cried the gardener. At that moment the queen's face rose and for the first time her eyes met those of the gardener. He instantly knew the answer. The queen had discovered the Rainbow Rose's only flaw; it had no scent. You see the queen was blind.

The story of the Rainbow Rose,[6] is a tale of expectations unfulfilled, of illusions and false hopes of one who is not seen

---

6Paraphrased from "The Rainbow Rose," in John Aurelio *Colors! Stories of the Kingdom* (New York: Crossroad, 1993), 14-16.

or unknown. Many passages of Scripture speak of this same idea. The Israelites, our ancestors in faith, had, as we know, an up and down relationship with God. The Book of Exodus (16:1-15) describes the complaints of the people to Moses and Aaron about their lack of food. They longed to return to Egypt, their place of bondage, so as to have their fill of food. Moses, as always intercedes for the people and God provides. But the expectations of the people were such that they did not recognize what God had provided for them. The people did not know what the manna was. Moreover, they were not able to recognize the hand of God in the miracle that had happened.

The Gospel of John (6:24-35) provides a similar story. The people have just been fed by Jesus; they had their fill. But Jesus brought much more than food for the body; He brought himself, the living bread. Like their ancestors, the Jews of Jesus' day did not understand; they did not recognize what Jesus brought. The Jews had a certain expectation of the Messiah and Redeemer. They wanted a ruler, like David, their father in faith; they wanted a liberator. Like the royal gardener, their expectations about Jesus were such that they were not able to accept what Jesus came to give them.

St. Paul also recognized this problem of the recognition of God in the many letters he wrote to the early Christian communities. In his Letter to the Ephesians (4:17-24) he tells the people that they must rethink their idea of who God is. Paul tells them to cast out illusions and false hopes of who God should or could be. Rather, he suggests that the people take a new view based on what Jesus said did. In other words, Paul is saying, step back, and look at your lives. Where has God come to us and we have failed to recognize him?

Recognition of God's presence in the world is not a problem which is isolated to people of earlier periods. In our ever more busy world which vies for our attention on all fronts at almost every moment, it is difficult to recognize Jesus, the one who must be our spiritual revolution. Expectations are a part of life in which we all participate; they are manifest in various ways. We have expectations of co-workers, neighbors, and associates. Our personal experience with these people dictates what our expectations will be. Expectations which are fulfilled do little for us. We assume these things; this is the way things are supposed to be! However, expectations which are unfulfilled raise red flags, create problems, and cause us to scurry about to find the person or thing that can meet our immediate need or expectation.

We place expectations on those who are most close and dear to us. We place expectations on members of our family, especially spouses and children. We even place expectations on God. Jesus says in John's Gospel (6:35), "I am the bread of life." What does this mean for us; what is out expectation? I think most of us would have to agree that at times we find in God what we want or think we need from God. Thus, the more probing question remains—can we accept God as he is manifest to us, especially in those most dear, and believe that in God's wisdom that which is provided is what we truly need?

How much will we risk, how far will we go to accept Jesus, our spiritual revolution? The Jews had to come to a completely new understanding of the Messiah in order to accept Jesus. Can we give a little so that Christ can come to us, especially in the faces of family and friends? Can we allow Jesus to be our spiritual revolution?

The royal gardener spent the majority of his life in an effort to develop the Rainbow Rose, a flower which could only be appreciated in a certain way. His high and rather narrow expectations of who the queen would be broke his heart. Jesus came and brought us all that we could possibly need. Still, he was rejected by many. The lot has now fallen to us. Let us strive to better accept Christ as he is manifested in those most dear. Let us allow Jesus to be our spiritual revolution this day.

Question: Am I often disappointed in people and events because my expectations are unrealistic?

Scripture Passage: "There is need of only one thing. Mary has chosen the better part, which will not be taken away from her." (Luke 10:42)

Prayer: Jesus, help me to be open to your presence and see you in my daily encounters of life.

Take Care—Be Ready

Narcissus and Goldmund, who were best friends, had met each other in the monastery called Mariabonn. Narcissus was a lay brother in the cloister, studying for ordination, and a teacher of Greek; Goldmund was a student. Narcissus was a man of discipline, patience and erudition; Goldmund was an impatient young man who needed to find himself in this world. The two friends talked about the Church, the subjects of scholarship, and their experiences in life. Goldmund wanted to become a member of the community of Mariabonn, possibly a teacher like his friend. But Narcissus knew that this would be impossible. Goldmund was a young man with neither faith nor direction in his life; he would never be ready for the unexpected in his life.

Goldmund left the monastery after completing his education and began a life of wandering. He traveled the land; he moved from town to town. He found himself moving from one experience of love to another. One day as he wandered he came across a knight. He attached himself to this man becoming a squire in the castle where the knight lived. Later he became an apprentice to a great sculptor in the town that adjoined the castle of the knight. The plague came to the town, however, and he was forced to flee and continue his journey from town to town. Whatever the situation Goldmund never seemed ready or prepared for what would happen.

Goldmund continued to wander for fifteen years or more. Without direction, lacking faith, he often thought about his friend Narcissus and a future time when they would, with God's help, see each other again.

One day Goldmund was accused and convicted of being a thief. He was brought before the royal magistrate of the town who sentenced him to death for his crime. The official gave Goldmund the opportunity to confess his sins to a priest before the sentence of death would be carried out. Goldmund, however, planned to use the opportunity to kill the priest, switch clothes, and make his escape. The plan of Goldmund was ready. The next day the priest came but Goldmund could not believe who entered his cell in the castle; the priest who came to hear his confession was Narcissus, his best friend. Goldmund's most trusted friend had returned, as he had many times longed for, but he was not ready.

This story told by the famous Austrian novelist Hermann Hesse well illustrates one of the important lessons taught by Jesus—be ready! The Lord makes his message crystal clear, "You also must be ready, for the Son of Man is coming at an unexpected hour." (Luke 12:40) The message of Jesus is appropriate for all of us when we think of those who enter our lives. Do we live our lives in a manner as if we are prepared for the unexpected person to enter? What is our motivation; are we ready?

When we speak to other people, do we do so in a manner which shows welcome to the person or would we be embarrassed if others heard our words? Do we live our lives with our family, friends, and business associates in a manner that gives welcome to Christ or would we be ashamed if the Lord knocked on the door of our heart and asked to enter?

How can we live our lives in such a way that shows welcome to the presence of God? The answer is found in the discovery of the significance of life, that is the meaning of life which is faith.

The Letter to the Hebrews tells us, "Now faith is the assurance of things hoped for, the conviction of things not seen." (11:1) If Goldmund had been a man of faith, he could have found the meaning, he could have been ready for the unexpected person in his life. Similarly, if we have faith, we will also be ready for the unexpected in our lives.

In the National Galley of London there hangs a famous painting with which many of us are familiar. In the work Christ stands in a garden; he is knocking on the front door to a small cottage in the garden. The scene is normal save one important detail; there is no handle on the door. The artist has described in paint what the Book of Revelation (3;20) states in words, "Listen! I am standing at the door, knocking; if you hear my voice and open the door, I will come in to you and eat with you, and you with me." The door has no handle because Jesus is knocking on the door to our hearts. Only we can open the door from the inside. The story of Narcissus and Goldmund and the lessons of Scripture challenge us to be ready for the presence of God in our life. Let us be ready to open to the presence of God; let us welcome the Lord this day!

Question: Is acceptance or anger my general reaction to the unexpected events of life?

Scripture Passage: "The Lord gave, and the Lord has taken away; blessed be the name of the Lord." (Job 1:21b)

Prayer: Lord, grant me the strength to accept your will for my life.

God Welcomes All

The "War to end all wars," the great World War I, created a problem of displaced persons that the world had never seen. In 1917 refugees and orphans abounded. Everywhere one turned the streets of cities and towns were filled with people who "did not belong." Because the war was fought in Europe, this human dilemma was greatest there, but that did not mean that things were fine here in the United States. For reasons that are very complicated this period of American history saw an alarming rise in the numbers of homeless children. Most were cast offs from homes. For reasons many times unknown children were released by parents and loved ones. They were forced to fend for themselves, to live on the streets as best as they were able to do. Nobody seemed to care about these children.

There was however, one who cared—his name was Edward Flanagan, a priest from New York. Father Flanagan decided that something needed to be done for the children of this country who were cast offs, who had been forced, for one reason or another, into a life on the streets. Flanagan purchased 1500 acres of land in eastern Nebraska near Omaha. He invited homeless boys, those rejected, those who had no one, to come to his new facility. No one was a foreigner or outsider to Edward Flanagan.

Starting in 1917 the little settlement began to grow. By 1936 the property had been incorporated into a village. By 1980 this village, known as Boys Town, a place for those who had nobody else, had over 600 residents.

The work of Father Edward Flanagan and his establishment of Boys Town illustrates the idea of how God accepts all, whoever we are, whatever we have done. Writing to the Hebrews after their return from exile in Babylon, Isaiah speaks of how God welcomes all people. Isaiah emphatically states that the people must do what is just; they must hold to God's law. "All who keep the Sabbath, and do not profane it, and hold fast my covenant—these I will bring to my mountain, and make them joyful in my house of prayer. (56:7a) Hebrews and foreigners are called by God. God's house is a house of prayer for all who choose to come. This certainly must have been a difficult teaching for the Hebrews to swallow—after all they were the chosen people. Now God says that all are welcome.

Matthew's Gospel (15:21-28) demonstrates how the mission of God has expanded to all people. A Canaanite woman asks Jesus for a favor, a miracle. Canaanites were outsiders; they lived east of the Jordan River. As foreigners they were not welcome. Jesus says that his mission is to the lost sheep of the House of Israel. In other words Jesus says his time is to be spent in bringing back the ten lost tribes of Israel; his mission is to the ancient Hebrews. The woman is persistent, however. Her perseverance and the cleverness of her response to Jesus' statement are rewarded. Jesus, through his action of curing the Canaanite woman's daughter, extends his mission, his ministry to all. Jesus accepts all; none are rejected. All people can receive the gifts of God.

Most certainly God welcomes us all. God created all and rejects nothing, no person, no thing. Parish communities of faith are good examples of how God accepts all. People come from different ethnic groups, are of different races, and have different states in life, and yet they gather together in prayer and work together in service. God accepts us for who we are today, not what we were yesterday, not what we will be tomorrow. God accepts us as we are, namely sinners struggling to further our relationship with God.

The only thing that can separate us from God is ourselves. In his Letter to the Romans St. Paul powerfully speaks of God's abundant mercy to all people. Paul says that the gifts and mercy of God are irrevocable. God has given us free will and with that gift we sometimes don't fully live up to our Christian calling; we are sinners. Yet, as Paul says, God made us in disobedience, imperfect in other words, so that he could show mercy to us. God wants to be merciful. His arms are open on the cross; he waits for our return. If we have failed it is because God created us as imperfect beings. There is nothing, absolutely nothing that God cannot forgive, except that for which we fail to ask forgiveness. St. Paul (Romans 8:38-39) says this so powerfully: "For I am convinced that neither death, nor life, nor angels, nor rulers, nor things present, nor things to come, nor powers, nor height, nor depth, nor anything else in all creation, will be able to separate us from the love of God in Christ Jesus our Lord."

Since God forgives and welcomes us we must do the same to those who enter our lives. We must be forgiving to those who hurt us, whether that be physically or psychologically. People will ignore us; this must be forgiven also. People at times will make our lives very difficult and uncomfortable. Jesus asks us to love them in return. Our task in life is to be bountiful in mercy to others and ourselves as God is with us.

Let us today welcome the foreigner, the refugee, the outcast. Let us in turn allow God to accept us. God the ever powerful and merciful one has gifts and forgiveness that can never be lost. Let us accept the loving embrace of God this day!

Question: What efforts do I make to welcome others as Christ welcomes us?

Scripture Passage: "For whoever does the will of my Father in heaven is my brother and sister and mother." (Matthew 12:50)
Prayer: Lord, help me always to find you in my sisters and brothers.

Piloting With God

"Red, right, returning." "Even red nuns have odd black cans." These expressions do not mean much to most people, but if you have ever navigated a ship safely from sea into port, these expressions are not only important, they may very well save your ship and the welfare of all onboard. Red, right, returning: red buoys are kept on the right or starboard side of your vessel when returning from sea. Even red nuns have odd black cans: in marking the channel all red "nun" type buoys have even numbers, while all black "can" type buoys have odd numbers.

The science of navigation, the discipline of moving from point A to point B safely, something usually associated with ships at sea, is a very sophisticated science. Today it is possible for the largest ocean going vessel or the smallest pleasure craft to determine at any place and time its precise position. The accuracy is remarkable, plus or minus a hundred yards. Considering the millions of square miles in the oceans of the world such precision is almost a miracle. This accuracy is possible through satellite navigation. When a ship approaches land, however, especially when it begins to enter port and navigate through the approach channel, even satellite navigation is not sufficiently accurate. The science of piloting is needed.

Piloting uses all kinds of guides to fix a ship's position. The piloting team of a navigator, plotter, and bearing taker uses buoys, lights, distinctive points of land, and ranges to determine the ship's precise location. It is imperative that the ship stay in the channel to avoid disaster. The piloting team, therefore, must follow the rules of the road, know the expressions like "red, right, returning," and especially follow the channel guides. If these aides are followed then most assuredly the vessel will arrive safely at berth. If not, the ship will find shoal water, run aground, and be as proverbially stated "in harms way."

Piloting a ship safely through the channel to a its berth is very much like navigating ourselves through the journey which is life. As we all now, life is anything but a straight line between birth and death. There are many turns—some are slight, some are major. Sometimes it seems like we are going back the way we originally came. The path of life has many challenges as well. Like the ship which must negotiate passed rocks or shoal water, so we must conquer disappointment, injury or sickness, death of family and friends, misunderstanding and a myriad of other problems we all face. Navigating through life is difficult, but we, like the ship, have guides to help us along the way. We have one another. When we affirm, challenge, or assist friends, neighbors or colleagues, we are serving as a guide to them. We have the Church. We have the Church's teachings, her tradition, and the Scriptures. Most especially we have God as our greatest and most reliable guide.

Scripture tells us how God has always been a guide to his people. The Pentateuch tells the story of how God guided the Hebrew people, who were uniquely God's own. Abraham, guided by God, journeyed from his native country to the land of Canaan. Moses and the Israelites were guided by God in their Exodus from Egypt. In fact, while in the desert God was manifest to the Hebrews in the form of a cloud by day and a pillar of fire by night. When the cloud or fire would advance so would the nation of Israel. We know, however, that the Hebrews did not follow the guides given to them. They had the Law, the Ten Commandments; they had God. Their failure to follow the guides provided resulted in their aimless wandering for forty years in the desert.

Jesus must be the premier guide in our lives. His message of peace, love, and forgiveness is a wonderful example, a guide by which we must live our lives. We remember Jesus' response when Thomas questioned him about the way, the proper path in life: "I am the way, the truth, and the life. No one comes to the Father except through me."(John 14:6) Jesus is the perfect guide in all things. Again Jesus emphasizes the need to place our total trust in his guiding hand. "I am the resurrection and the life. Those who believe in me, even though they die will live, and everyone who lives and believes in me will never die." (John 11:26). Trust me, Jesus says, and I will lead you home. Jesus will guide us safely to eternal life.

Our lives are complicated; they are full of turns, challenges, and obstacles. But God has given us the guides that we need to safely arrive where we want to go. We have each other; we have the Church. Most especially we have the Son, Jesus. As we walk the road of life, let us remember to use the guides we have been given. If we fail in this task the challenges of life will destroy us and we will be lost. If we allow Jesus to be our pilot, however, our final berth will be with God, the one who brings us to salvation and eternal life.

Question: What signs do I follow in life, those of the world or those of God?

Scripture Passage: "I am the way, and the truth, and the life. No one comes to he Father except through me." (John 14:6)

Prayer: Lord, help me to follow the path that leads to eternal life.

God's Word Blossoms Forth

"Sticks and stones may break my bones, but words can never hurt me." When we were children our mothers told us this expression to ward off any bad feeling we might experience from the cruelty which can many times come from the mouths of children. It may be true that words cannot physically harm us, but words can and do have a great influence in our lives. Sometimes the effect is injurious to character and mind; other times the effect is positive and brings us to new heights. The power of words is at our command; we must use it wisely.

Our world is dominated by words. The vast majority of all communication is by words. We speak to some people and listen to others in order to exchange information. We read the paper to discover the current events; novels take us to far off lands without leaving the comfort of our easy chair. Words can be destructive of character or person; we can libel or slander someone with our words. Words can also express our love, encouragement, or gratefulness. Words play such an important role, but they do so only when they are taken inside our person, are contemplated, mentally digested, and become a part of us.

The ability of the God's word to influence and feed us as humans is clearly seen in Scripture. The image in Isaiah the prophet is quite vivid. "For as the rain and the snow came down from heaven, and do not return there until they have watered the earth, making it bring forth and sprout,...so shall my word be that goes out from my mouth; it shall not return to me empty, but it shall accomplish that which I purpose and succeed in the thing for which I sent it." (55:10a, 11). As the rains from the sky water the earth and produce an abundance, so must God's word be taken into us so that it can nurture us. Then we can blossom forth in a rich harvest.

Many times, however, God's word encounters severe obstacles in our society. The Gospel parable of the sower (Matthew 13:1-9) describes many of these pitfalls. God, the sower, provides the word, the seed. God is ever faithful and vigilant in this task. We, the receivers, however, are not always as receptive as we should be. Sometimes, as the parable points out, God's word comes to us, but we are not interested and thus the word is stolen from us by another. At other times God's word comes and we receive it with joy. But the word is received superficially; it is not properly rooted. Thus, when stimulated the word sprouts quickly, but it withers and fades with equal rapidity. There are times as well that the word of God gets choked off by the cares of this world. It may be another person, something of our material world or even possibly our own perceived self-importance. In such cases the word has no place to grow and later be harvested; it is ignored. Fortunately there are those special times when God's word is received, it enters fully into us and we blossom forth thirty, sixty, or one hundred fold.

Our task is to allow God's word which comes to us to penetrate and sink deep down. Here it makes a difference and begins to grow. God's word must be primary in our life. It cannot be something we think about now and then; it cannot be something that is on the outside. God's word must enter in so as to nurture us. Then and only then can God create something beautiful in us.

Where can we find God's word? There are many places where God's word abounds, but three important ones come to mind. God's word is first found in Scripture. When we attend Mass do we listen to the readings and reflect upon them or do we merely hear what is proclaimed with little attention being paid? When we are home do we take the opportunity to read the Bible? More importantly do we take time to mediate on God's word? God's word is also found in prayer. Most Christians are people of prayer. We verbalize our needs to God many times each day. Prayer, however, is a conversation between God and humans. Any good conversation is two way and thus we must listen to God as well. God's word also comes in the challenges of family members, friends, and colleagues. Do we listen to what people have to say to us, or do we sort of shrug off what others say? Do we give others a chance to speak, or are we so busy talking that our family, friends, and colleagues cannot get a word in edgewise?

God's word is all around. Like the rain, however, unless it penetrates and nurtures us it can do little good. But if it does nurture us, then we will find resurrection. We have God's promise on that. St. Paul writes to the Christian community at Corinth and says that we have no idea of the glory that will one day be ours: "What no eye has seen, nor ear heard, nor the human heart conceived, what God has prepared for those who love him." (I Corinthians 2:9)

Let us allow God's word to water and nurture us. Like the rains that water the earth, so may God's word penetrate and nurture us along the way. With the power of God's word we will blossom forth, produce a rich harvest, and in the end find resurrection and eternal life.

Question: How faithful am I to my daily conversation with God?

Scripture Passage: "Lord, teach us to pray, as John taught his disciples." (Luke 11:1b)

Prayer: Lord, make me more prayerful and grateful for your presence in my life.

Acting on Our Belief

"Who do people say the Son of Man is?" Jesus asked this question of those who knew him best, his chosen followers. The responses he received varied: "Some say John the Baptist, others Elijah, still others one of the prophets." Jesus then asked, "But who do you say I am?" Peter, the one along with his brother Andrew who had first received the call, answered in faith, "You are the Messiah, the Son of the living God." (Matthew 16:14-16) Peter's answer was not attainable by any human means—that is why Jesus tells him that this revelation came from God. Peter's declaration was not an isolated comment made and then forgotten. Although it took time and did not reach its full potential until Pentecost, Peter's confession of faith became the source from which he drew strength. Peter acted on his belief; we must do the same.

Daily life calls us to action and many times what we do serves to impress those who enter, influence, and even control our lives. It seems that we will do almost anything if our actions will get us where we want to go. Personal relationships and love are powerful incentives which motivate people to action. When two people meet and fall in love a new set of rules seems to govern what one will do for another. People in love will go out of their way for the other so as to maximize time together and make the all-important impression which helps to bring the relationship to greater wholeness. Suddenly people become more free with time and money and they find the ability to enjoy new things and places, all because of a special person. Working people, consciously and unconsciously, do what is necessary to get along with colleagues and supervisors. When the boss holds the cards for pay incentives and promotions, workers often do "what is necessary" to assure themselves of a better future. This action of meeting the expectations of others is also found in sports when athletically-gifted people take the road which will draw the coach's attention and, thereby, get them more playing time, notice, and possible accolades.

Working hard so as to maximize our possibilities in relationships, work, sports, and other aspects of life is a blessing for it demonstrates our incentive, especially to set goals and achieve them. For a motivated person it is possible, even rather easy, to increase our efforts for people we can see and goals that stand before us. Can we act in an equally motivated and excited manner about doing what God asks of us, knowing through faith that what we do will bring us the greatest prize of all? St. Paul knew that the goal, life on high with Jesus, was worthy of his efforts and thus he raced to the finish line, fighting the good fight and winning the race (II Timothy 4:7). It was his unseen vision which kept him going: "What no eye has seen, not ear heard, not the human heart conceived, what God has prepared for those who love him." (I Corinthians 2:9)

We who profess the belief, as did Peter, that Jesus is the Messiah, the Son of the living God, should do all that we can to welcome the unseen God and to act on our belief. To act on that which can be seen is relatively simple, but it is equally easy to by-pass that which in invisible. To take time for that special person, our work, or other projects which effect us directly comes almost naturally, but how difficult it is to go out of our way for God. Jesus, during his life of earth did not seem to have any difficulty going out of his way for all of us. In his famous Christological hymn in Philippians (2:6-11), St.

Paul says that even though Jesus knew himself to be God he did not deem equality with God, but rather embraced human form and accepted death on the cross. Jesus acted on his belief and knowledge of the Father and he did it for the unseen billions who would follow in future generations. Jesus acted for us; can we act for him?

When Jesus ascended to heaven after the resurrection, the world was deprived of his physical presence, but Jesus did not abandon us. On the contrary, he promised that he would be with us until the end of the world (Matt 28:20) and he sent the Holy Spirit on Pentecost to enlighten and strengthen us while dispelling doubt and fear. Jesus is physically present, but he masks himself in you and me. For those who have opened their hearts to the Lord, Jesus has taken residence. We have thus become the hands, feet, and eyes of the Lord which gives us a great responsibility along with a privilege. Christ acted for those whom he knew and others he did not. As the vehicles of Christ in the world we must do the same. Working to build the Kingdom of God may not bring economic dividends, influential friends, high position, or status in this life, but it will reap spiritual benefits today and the fullness of life tomorrow.

Acting on our belief in Christ is not easy, but it must be the central activity of our lives. Peter's profession of faith in Jesus was only the first step in his movement to union with God; it was necessary to act on his belief. Christians by name, symbol, and word profess their belief in Jesus as well. Let us be aware of the need for greater faith in our lives; let us profess and act upon what we believe.

Question: Do my words and actions clearly demonstrate my profession that Jesus is Lord?

Scripture Passage: "Do whatever they [the Pharisees] teach you and follow it; but do not do as they do, for they do not practice what they teach." (Matthew 23:3)

Prayer: Jesus, help me to never deny you in what I say or do.

God is Present in All that We Do

Few Americans today remember Samuel Provoost. This is a shame for his courage in the face of opposition, especially during a time of national crisis, will not soon be forgotten. Provoost was born in New York City in 1742 and was raised in the Reformed tradition of John Calvin. Like many young men in the American colonies in those days, he was sent to England to complete his education. While he was there he experienced a form of religious conversion. He began to understand God in a new and different way. He rejected the fatalism and predestination of Calvinism and adopted the more positive human anthropology offered by the Anglican communion. Encouraged by his friends, he entered a seminary after his preparatory education was finished and was eventually ordained a priest in 1766.

That same year Provoost returned to his native colony of New York and was installed as the vice rector of Trinity Church in New York City. At that time in the colonies the cry of revolution could be heard on many fronts. In the early 1770s the Sugar and Stamp Acts, Boston Tea Party, and other events were the catalyst behind Patrick Henry's famous words, "Give me liberty or give me death!" Yes, the cry of liberty, freedom, and revolution was in the air. Samuel Provoost became caught up in the American drive for independence. He experienced a major obstacle in his belief, however, from the parishioners at Trinity Church. The people, especially the electors, felt their priest should not be involved with the political activities of the colonies; his mission was to handle religious questions in the Church. Samuel Provoost, however, believed something quite different. He had come to believe in faith that all he had was gift. His life, his new found Anglican communion, his position, the opportunities he had been given, even his material possessions were gifts from God. Since all came from God, all must be of God as well. God could not be sequestered into a church building on Sunday morning alone. No, God must be found in all aspects of life, including the American drive for freedom. The pressure from the electors, however, became too great for Provoost. In order not to cause public scandal he resigned his position at Trinity.

Provoost's resignation did not silence his speech or his pen, however. He traveled about extensively, especially in the northern colonies, speaking with anyone who would listen and he wrote many essays and editorials in local newspapers, all in advocacy of the American cause of liberty. After the signing of the Declaration of Independence and the first few years of the war, Provoost became well known throughout the new United States of America through his courageous stand for the nation.

In 1784 the electors of Trinity parish, themselves having experienced some form of conversion, invited Samuel Provoost back to their community—this time as rector or pastor. Provoost dove into his new responsibilities with full vigor, both the pastoral work and his continued support for the American revolutionary cause. Additionally, he was asked to begin the formal organization of the Episcopal Church in the new nation. The United States also recognized the contribution of Samuel Provoost. In 1785 Provoost was appointed the first chaplain of the Continental Congress. Samuel Provoost believed in the presence of God in all aspects of life. In thought and ministry he was able to demonstrate that his belief was true.

Do we recognize the presence of God in all that we do? Scripture challenges us to reflect upon this question and respond. Matthew's account of Jesus' encounter with the Pharisees and Herodians on the payment of tax (22:15-21) presents an interesting case. On first reading, it appears that Jesus is describing the need to divide our world into two neatly packaged and distinct categories or divisions, the sacred and the secular. "'Tell us then, what do you think. Is it lawful to pay taxes to the emperor or not?' But Jesus, aware of their malice, said, 'Why are you putting me to the test, you hypocrites? Show me the coin used for the tax.' And they brought him a *denarius*. Then he said to them, 'Whose head is this, and whose title?' They answered, 'The emperor's.' Then he said to them, 'Give therefore to the emperor the things that are the emperor's and to God the things that are God's.'" (Matthew 22:17-21) The pharisees, who were Jewish nationalists, represent the sacred realm. They did not believe in rendering tribute to the emperor, namely Caesar. The Herodians, who were Roman sympathizers, represent the secular world. They strongly believed that tribute should be given to the Emperor. Jesus, caught in the middle, presents his clever compromise. What, however, belongs to Caesar and what belongs to God? It seems in the story that the coin, with the inscription of Caesar's likeness, represents the secular world and must be given to the Emperor. Jesus, however, never says exactly what belongs to Caesar and what belongs to God. If we believe like Samuel Provoost that all has its origin in God and thus all is of God, then there is no separation between the sacred and secular. Rather these two ideas represent a fundamental unity.

The prophet Isaiah demonstrates the truth of this statement. God, speaking through the prophet, says to Cyrus, the liberator of Israel from Babylon, " I call you by name, I surname you, though you do not know me....I arm you, though you do not know me,...I form the light and create the darkness, I make weal and create woe: I the Lord do all these things." (45:4b,5b,7). All that Cyrus had came from God.

Since God is the source of all things, there is a natural human desire to reciprocate, to give back to God. We respond to God, not out of duty, but because God first loved us, called us, chose us, and, as St. Paul says in his writings, will lead us to glory. Paul applauds the Christian community at Thessalonica for its "work of faith and labor of love and steadfastness of hope in our Lord Jesus Christ." (1:3b). As God has given fully to the Thessalonians, so Paul tells the people to place God in all that they do and say. The same must be true for all of us.

We must recognize the presence of God in all things. The way we live our lives must be an expression of the faith and hope that we possess. The world that God gave us is a wonderful place. Certainly there are problems; the world is incomplete. At times bad things happen to good people. But through it all God's creation stands as something good and worthy of our effort. We should always enjoy what God has given to us. We should maximize our potential in the world and its possibilities for us. We must make the world a better place for those who will follow in our footsteps.

With all that the world demands of us there certainly is a need to develop different techniques for the various things we do. Different situations require different methods. Yet, it is fundamentally important that the rules we use in making decisions never change. If our efforts are required in the community, at church, or in the business world, the rule that God must be present can never be forgotten. When we are required to handle delicate or difficult situations with people, whether they be members of our family, business associates, or even strangers, we again can never forget God. God must be central and integral to all that we do and say.

Lived in an attitude of thanksgiving our lives must manifest the presence of God. Although it is difficult to do, because we are trained to do the opposite, we must avoid the temptation to divide our world into neat and orderly categories of the sacred and the secular. All power, wealth, position, and opportunity come from God. Since God is in all, we must take the presence of God inside each of us and apply it to all that we do. Samuel Provoost was a man who was able to manifest the presence of God in his belief and his actions, showing God's presence in all aspects of his life. Mary, the mother of God, magnified the presence of God in all that she said and did. Her words, recorded by Luke the Evangelist (1:46-49), say it all: "My soul magnifies the Lord, and my spirit rejoices in God my Savior, for he has looked with favor on the lowliness of his servant. Surely, from now on generations will call me blessed; for the Mighty One has done great things for me and holy in his name." Let us believe and act the same!

Question: Where do I seek and find the presence of God?

Scripture Passage: "[Jesus said] And remember, I am with you always, to the end of the age." (Matthew 28:20b)

Prayer: Lord God, help me to find your creative, redemptive and sanctifying presence in all things.

Those Who Seek the Truth Hear God's Voice

The International Government of the World or IGW made its announcement with joy: the last Christian in the world was dead. This last Christian was found hiding in an abandoned mine in South Africa. He was ferreted out, brought to trial, convicted, and then executed, all the while professing Christ. The world state ordered a half-day international holiday to celebrate. The rejoicing grew to a fever pitch. Images of Christ on the Cross were burned in sub-capitals throughout the world and singing, which had been banned for more than a century, was permitted this one time to aid the celebration.

Yes, it was a sad and strange day which witnessed these events. The rulers of the IGW were the sons and daughters of those who a century early has crushed truth, eliminated all rebellious peoples, and subjected humans to the monster machines of the age. The founders of the world state had created their empire by the elimination of all adversaries, all ideas, peoples, institutions, and religions. A chemist at that time had discovered a way to combine fuel, food, and water so that it was possible with the resultant mixture to control an entire population with a cadre of six. A special gas was developed which destroyed all the fertile land in the world. All vegetation, all trees, plants, fruits and flowers were destroyed. Even to consider cultivation of these was punishable by death. People no longer had names; they were given numbers. Any children born were raised by the IGW. Those who were intelligent or asked questions were eliminated. The whole world population was subdued and made obedient slaves by the production of one common food for all. It was a thick liquid that was piped into each person's cell; there were no homes. All trains, planes, automobiles, and people operated on the same fuel.

There was, however, an imperfection in the IGW. This Godless society of the anti-Christ which had crushed out all truth had a weakness. The weak link was present in the form of a little wiry man, #2,750,300. He lived in the world capital, SC1, a city formerly called New York. Now #2,750,300 was a bit different than other slaves; he possessed a twinkle in his eye. Still, he carried the proper credentials and thus was not eliminated by the IGW. Actually #2,750,300, whom we can call Mr. White for short, was a model slave. He did his duty well; he was above all suspicion. On Restday, Sunday no longer existed, Mr. White many times left SC1, but where he went no one was certain. He often went to a rural section of the land where one day he found something quite remarkable, a piece of brown earth which had not been destroyed; it was his oasis.

One Restday in the spring Mr. White journeyed to this little plot of earth. He brought with him a packet which he emptied onto the soil. The moist earth gladly welcomed the offering given to it. "I will bring God back to the world," thought #2,750,300. He left and returned home.

Time passed; spring and summer came and went. One fall day, that season that in earlier centuries was so beautiful when trees existed on earth, Mr. White went to his plot of land. There blowing in the gentle breeze was a crop of wheat. The fact that the IGW had never discovered the plot was a minor miracle. White hurriedly harvested his crop, pounded the grain, and formed it. Using the stubble of the wheat he built a fire and baked the wheat. The yield was two small wafers. He took his prize home to await his day.

Several weeks later, early one morning, Mr. White arose. He gathered his precious wafers and pulled out a box from under his bed that had remained undetected by the IGW officials. Gathering his things he made his way out into the street and across town. In this early morning hour all was still; the slaves were asleep. He entered the tallest building in the world, found the elevator, and pushed the button for the top floor, more than one-half mile up in the sky. When he arrived on the roof, White disabled the elevator, so no one could follow, set up a table, and pulled from his box an ornate cup and plate, two cruets, one with a clear liquid and one with a red substance, and some odd-looking clothes. Yes, there still was one Christian in the world; the last Christian was a priest. When the first rays of dawn were seen in the eastern sky the Mass began. A small plane happened to fly close to the building. The pilot observed the scene, and remembering from his history lessons, realized what was happening. He radioed the IGW headquarters; the master was informed. "The Mass must be stopped; it must be stopped," he cried. Planes were sent, bombs were dropped, gunfire was applied, but the Mass continued. Then the words were spoken "This is my body, given for you." With that a crack of thunder was heard and a streak of lightning flashed through the sky. The clouds parted and in the distance Christ could be seen coming toward earth. Yes, it was the end of the world. Jesus had come to claim his own and restore truth to the world.

Myles Connelly tells this story in his 1928 novelette, *Mr. Blue*. It provides us the opportunity to reflect upon truth in our life and our need to act so as to prepare the world for Christ's return.

I am sure that all people are amazed, even at a loss, when they contemplate the power and awesomeness of God. The Prophet Daniel (7:13-14) illustrates this point through his vision of how all peoples, nations and languages are subject to God. God's reign will last forever. The author of the Book of Revelation (1:5-8) speaks of God as the Alpha and the Omega, the one who is and who is to come, the Almighty. How can we who are finite people comprehend the power of God? The answer must be that we need to elevate our minds and hearts; we need to reach a different plane. We need to seek the truth. Christ's kingship was not what was expected; He brought a kingship of truth. We can seek the truth for as Jesus says in the Gospel (John 18:37), in answering Pilate's question, "I was born, I came into the world for one purpose—to bear witness to the truth."

Sacred Scripture presents us with a great challenge, but it also gives us a wonderful promise. The challenge can succinctly be put in this way: How do we seek the truth? What is the truth and where will we find it? In order to seek the truth we must elevate our minds and our hearts. We need to reach for the higher realms of which St. Paul speaks in his writings. We must begin the search by looking inside, by meditation and reflection. This is a good start. When will we know that we have found God? The answer will be different for each person; such a task involves much self-discovery. But one thing is certain—when we find God we will know the truth and when we know the truth we will discover God. Yes, God is the truth.

Seeking the truth is not easy; it requires much effort on our part. We do not live in a world state run by the IGW, but we would be foolish to think that society today readily accepts the presence of God or God's truth. Therefore, we must be #2,750,300. We must take the risks to seek the truth and we must act on what we find. We must do our share to bring Christ back to our world.

Yes, there is a great challenge, but there is a promise as well. Jesus says, "Everyone who belongs to the truth listens to my voice." Our sincere efforts will be rewarded; there can be little doubt. In discovering truth we bring the world and all its inhabitants one step closer to the purpose for which we all live—to welcome Christ when he returns to claim the world. Yes, there is a promise tomorrow; it is the goal for which we daily strive—eternal life. But there is a promise today as well. As Scripture puts it, "Know the truth and the truth will make you free." (John 8:32)

Question: Do I embrace the truth that is God or seek false avenues?

Scripture Passage: "If you continue in my word, you will truly be my disciples; and you will know the truth, and the truth will make you free." (John 8:31b-32)

Prayer: Father, help me to follow your Son, the way, the truth and the life.

Manufactured By: RR Donnelley
Momence, IL USA
January, 2011